Bananas, Smartphones, and Gasoline:

The Global Journey of Everyday Things

Dr. Steven Fawkes

© Steven Fawkes 2024

Published by EP Strategy Ltd

ISBN: 979 8 34055 442 0

Bananas, Smartphones, and Gasoline: The Global Journey of Everyday Things

Table of Contents

The World in Your Pocket *1*

Part 1: Bananas – The Story of Global Agriculture *6*

Chapter 1: A Brief History of Bananas *6*

Chapter 2: The Banana Empire *11*

Chapter 3: The Environmental Cost of Bananas *20*

Part 2: Smartphones – The Digital Revolution *29*

Chapter 4: From Sand to Silicon: Building a Smartphone *29*

Chapter 5: The Rise of the Smartphone Era *39*

Chapter 6: E-Waste and the Problem of Planned Obsolescence *48*

Part 3: Gasoline – Fueling the Modern World *56*

Chapter 7: The Discovery of Oil and the Birth of Gasoline *56*

Chapter 8: The Geopolitics of Oil *63*

Chapter 9: The Environmental Impact of Gasoline *71*

Part 4: The Future of Bananas, Smartphones, and Gasoline *79*

Chapter 10: The Future of Food: Sustainable Bananas *79*

Chapter 11: The Smartphone of Tomorrow *86*

Chapter 12: Beyond Gasoline: The Energy Transition *93*

Conclusion: The Invisible Threads Connecting Us *101*

Glossary of Terms: Bananas, Smart Phones, and Gasoline *106*

Resources for Further Reading: Bananas, Smart Phones, and Gasoline *112*

Index for Bananas, Smart Phones, and Gasoline *117*

About the author: Dr. Steven Fawkes *119*

The World in Your Pocket

In our fast-paced, modern world, it's easy to overlook the everyday objects that surround us—bananas ripening in the fruit bowl, a smartphone buzzing on the table, a car filling up at the gas station. We rarely pause to consider how these familiar items arrive in our lives or the immense forces behind their existence. Each of these objects—bananas, smartphones, and gasoline—embodies the power of global trade, technological advancement, and resource consumption. Through their journeys from production to consumption, they reveal the vast and often invisible networks that connect our world.

This book, *Bananas, Smartphones, and Gasoline*, aims to uncover these hidden systems. By tracing the paths of these three seemingly unrelated objects, we can see how agriculture, technology, and energy intersect to shape the global economy, influence political decisions, and impact the environment. Bananas, smartphones, and gasoline serve as metaphors for larger forces at play in our daily lives—forces that, though often unseen, dictate much of the modern experience.

From the jungles of Central America to the factories of China, from oil-rich nations to the world's busiest ports, these objects are not just commodities. They are stories of human ingenuity, exploitation, innovation, and survival. Through their journey, this book offers an in-depth exploration of how the products we rely on are part of an intricate web of global systems, showing us that our world has become interconnected in ways that previous generations could hardly have imagined.

The Global Network of Everyday Products

The world has become a vast network of interconnected products. The banana you enjoy for breakfast might have travelled thousands of miles from a plantation in Ecuador, ripened on a cargo ship crossing the Panama Canal, and made its way to your local supermarket just in time for you to buy it. The smartphone in your hand contains components sourced from dozens of countries, where materials like cobalt, lithium, and rare earth metals are mined, processed, and assembled by a global workforce before the device reaches your pocket.

Gasoline, meanwhile, fuels your car, having originated from crude oil extracted from deep beneath the earth's surface, often in politically volatile regions. These commodities are emblematic of the complex global trade routes that connect every corner of the planet.

In the modern world, these products are not isolated items, but rather components of a much larger and deeply interconnected global system. The journey of a banana from farm to supermarket shelf involves far more than agricultural processes—it touches on economics, trade regulations, shipping logistics, and even the environmental consequences of monoculture farming. Likewise, the production of smartphones depends on a supply chain that spans the globe, involving raw material extraction, labour practices, technological advancements, and international trade policies. Gasoline, one of the most politically charged commodities, reflects the complexities of energy consumption, geopolitics, and the delicate balance between the world's dependency on fossil fuels and the urgent need for sustainable alternatives.

The goal of this book is to peel back the layers of these global systems to reveal the intricate connections behind everyday products. By focusing on three key objects—bananas, smartphones, and gasoline—we can understand how our daily choices are shaped by forces beyond our immediate awareness. In a world that is more interconnected than ever before, these objects offer a window into the economic, environmental, and social factors that define the 21st century.

Bananas: The Global Fruit

Bananas, the most traded fruit in the world, provide a perfect case study for understanding the intricacies of global agriculture and trade. This simple, yellow fruit has become a staple in many households, but its journey from tropical plantations to grocery stores is far from simple.

In Part 1 of this book, we'll explore the origins of bananas in Southeast Asia and their spread to Central and South America, where they are now grown on massive industrial plantations. Bananas symbolize the complex interplay between agriculture and global trade, as well as the environmental and social consequences of monoculture farming. Behind every banana lies a hidden story of labour exploitation, land use, and environmental degradation, all driven by the demand for cheap, accessible fruit in wealthier nations.

We'll look at how major corporations, such as United Fruit (now Chiquita), have dominated the banana trade for over a century, shaping the economies and politics of entire regions. These companies have been responsible for both the rise of "banana republics" and for wielding immense power over labour conditions, land ownership, and government policy in Latin America. Additionally, the environmental impact of banana farming, including deforestation and the use of harmful pesticides, raises questions about sustainability and the long-term future of global agriculture.

Through the story of bananas, we'll examine how agriculture is not just a local or national issue but a global one, with far-reaching consequences for economies, societies, and ecosystems. The banana's journey reveals the global supply chains and trade networks that bring food to our tables, exposing the vulnerabilities and challenges inherent in our current agricultural systems.

Smartphones: The Technology of Connection

Smartphones, the quintessential product of the digital age, are far more than just sleek, powerful devices. They represent the cutting edge of technology and the triumph of globalization, but they also embody the complexities of modern manufacturing, resource extraction, and labour practices.

In Part 2, we will dive into the world of smartphones, tracing their journey from raw materials to finished products. The production of smartphones depends on a wide array of components, including metals like cobalt and lithium, which are often mined in challenging and dangerous conditions in countries like the Democratic Republic of the Congo and Chile. The extraction of these resources, often involving child labour and poor working conditions, highlights the dark side of global supply chains.

From there, the story moves to China, where the majority of smartphones are assembled. We'll explore the rise of factories like Foxconn, where workers toil in highly controlled environments to meet the insatiable demand for new devices. The smartphone industry's emphasis on planned obsolescence—where devices are designed to be replaced rather than repaired—fuels a cycle of consumption that generates enormous amounts of electronic waste, posing significant environmental challenges.

Smartphones also serve as a powerful metaphor for the interconnectedness of the modern world. These devices allow us to communicate instantly with people across the globe, access vast amounts of information, and participate in global economies, yet they also remind us of the inequalities and environmental costs embedded in the technology we rely on. In this section, we'll investigate how smartphones shape our lives and how their production reflects the broader dynamics of globalization, consumption, and labour exploitation.

Gasoline: Fueling the Modern World

Gasoline, the lifeblood of modern economies, represents the global energy system and its dependence on fossil fuels. Its journey, from extraction to combustion, tells a story of geopolitics, economic power, and environmental degradation.

In Part 3, we'll explore the origins of gasoline, beginning with the discovery of oil and the development of the internal combustion engine. We'll trace the rise of the oil industry, which has transformed economies, shaped global politics, and sparked numerous conflicts. Oil-rich nations, from the Middle East to Venezuela, have long wielded considerable power on the world stage, using their vast reserves to influence international policy and maintain control over energy supplies.

The environmental consequences of gasoline consumption are undeniable. As one of the leading contributors to climate change, gasoline-powered vehicles are at the centre of the global debate on sustainability and the need for renewable energy sources. This section will examine the environmental costs of our reliance on gasoline and explore the potential for alternative energy solutions, such as electric vehicles and renewable fuels. We will also discuss the geopolitical complexities of transitioning away from fossil fuels and the economic challenges that come with reshaping global energy systems.

Gasoline's journey reveals the intricate connections between energy, politics, and the environment, illustrating how one commodity can hold such sway over the course of human history. By understanding the role of gasoline in our world, we gain insight into the broader issues of energy consumption, climate change, and the future of global sustainability.

Structure of the Book

Bananas, Smartphones, and Gasoline is structured into three main parts, each dedicated to one of the key objects at the centre of our modern world: bananas, smartphones, and gasoline - each representing three critical systems; agriculture; technology; and energy. Each part begins with the origins of these products, tracing their historical development and their integration into global trade systems. From there, the book delves into the social, economic, and environmental impacts of their production and consumption, illustrating the far-reaching consequences of these industries.

Through detailed analysis, interviews with experts, and on-the-ground reporting, this book seeks to provide readers with a comprehensive understanding of how these everyday objects connect us to global systems. The chapters move seamlessly from the personal to the global, showing how the choices we make as consumers are linked to larger forces that shape the world we live in.

Conclusion: Our Shared Future

Bananas, Smartphones, and Gasoline offers a glimpse into the hidden systems that shape our lives and a reminder that the products we consume every day are not isolated items but are deeply interconnected with the world around us. These objects serve as metaphors for the larger forces of agriculture, technology, and energy that drive global economies, influence political decisions, and impact the environment.

By tracing the journeys of bananas, smartphones, and gasoline, this book invites readers to reflect on their role in these global systems and to consider how their choices can contribute to a more sustainable, equitable future. In the pages that follow, we'll uncover the world in your pocket and reveal the interconnected nature of our modern lives.

Part 1: Bananas – The Story of Global Agriculture

Chapter 1: A Brief History of Bananas

Bananas are a ubiquitous fruit, found in markets, supermarkets, and kitchens around the globe. Their sweet, soft flesh and convenient packaging make them a favorite snack, while their affordability and nutritional value have elevated them to the status of a global staple. But behind the banana's everyday presence lies a rich and complex history that spans thousands of years. From its origins in the tropical rainforests of Southeast Asia to its evolution as the world's most traded fruit, the story of the banana is a fascinating journey of domestication, migration, and industrialization.

Origins of Bananas and Their Domestication

The journey of the banana begins over 7,000 years ago in the dense tropical rainforests of Southeast Asia, particularly in what is now Malaysia, Indonesia, and the Philippines. Wild bananas, known scientifically as *Musa acuminata* and *Musa balbisiana*, were among the earliest plant species to be domesticated by humans in this region. These wild varieties were very different from the modern banana we know today; they were filled with large, hard seeds and had a much tougher texture.

The domestication of bananas involved a complex process of selecting and breeding banana plants with desirable traits. Early farmers began to cultivate bananas that exhibited mutations resulting in seedless, more palatable fruits. The earliest domesticated bananas were likely hybrids between the *Musa acuminata* and *Musa balbisiana* species, which produced fruit with fewer seeds and a higher flesh-to-seed ratio. These early bananas would have been an important food source due to their nutritional content, providing carbohydrates, potassium, and vitamins essential for human health.

As human populations grew and migrated, so did bananas. From their origins in Southeast Asia, bananas spread to the islands of the Pacific, including Papua New Guinea and the Solomon Islands. Archaeological evidence suggests that bananas were being cultivated in

Papua New Guinea as early as 5,000 BCE, making it one of the first regions outside Southeast Asia to engage in banana farming. The spread of bananas to these regions was likely facilitated by early seafaring communities who transported banana saplings and cuttings across the ocean.

As a domesticated crop, bananas were well-suited to the tropical climates of Southeast Asia and the Pacific, where they thrived in the warm, humid conditions. Over time, bananas became deeply integrated into the diets and agricultural practices of the communities that cultivated them. This early history of bananas, rooted in selective breeding and geographic expansion, laid the foundation for their eventual global journey.

Role of Bananas in the Diets of Ancient Civilizations

As bananas spread across Southeast Asia and into the Pacific Islands, they became a staple crop for many ancient civilizations. Their ability to grow in diverse tropical environments, their high nutritional value, and their adaptability to different soil conditions made bananas an essential part of the diet in these regions.

One of the most notable early uses of bananas was in the ancient civilizations of India. By the time bananas reached the Indian subcontinent, they were already an established and valued food source. Historical texts, such as the *Pali Canon* (Buddhist scriptures), refer to the consumption of bananas in India as early as 600 BCE. Ancient Hindu texts also mention bananas, highlighting their significance in the region's agricultural and culinary traditions. In India, bananas were not only consumed as food but were also imbued with cultural and religious importance. The banana plant, with its large green leaves and abundant fruit, became associated with fertility, prosperity, and auspiciousness in Hindu rituals.

From India, bananas made their way to the Middle East, where they were cultivated and consumed by various ancient civilizations. Alexander the Great, during his conquest of India in 327 BCE, is said to have encountered bananas and brought them back to the Mediterranean region. By this time, bananas had already begun to spread westward along trade routes, thanks to Arab traders who carried the fruit across the Indian Ocean to Africa and the Middle East.

In Africa, bananas became a vital crop for many early civilizations. The tropical climate of sub-Saharan Africa provided ideal conditions for banana cultivation, and the fruit quickly became integrated into the agricultural systems of regions such as East Africa. Bananas are believed to have arrived in Africa around the first millennium CE, where they became an essential food source for the Bantu-speaking peoples of Central and East Africa. In these regions, bananas were not only consumed fresh but were also used to make beer, an important cultural practice that persists in many African communities to this day.

In addition to their importance as a food source, bananas played a role in the social and economic life of these ancient civilizations. Bananas were traded along ancient routes, exchanged between communities, and incorporated into local economies. Their ease of cultivation and relatively high yield made them an attractive crop for both subsistence and trade, further cementing their status as a staple food in many parts of the ancient world.

The Transformation of the Banana into a Global Commodity

While bananas had already spread across much of Southeast Asia, Africa, and the Middle East by the early centuries of the common era, their transformation into a truly global commodity did not occur until the rise of European colonialism and the advent of global trade networks in the 19th century.

The European discovery of bananas came much later than other civilizations. Christopher Columbus is often credited with introducing bananas to the Western world when he encountered them during his second voyage to the Caribbean in 1493. Columbus brought banana plants back to Europe, but the fruit remained relatively unknown on the continent for several centuries. It wasn't until the late 1800s, with the expansion of European colonial empires and advances in transportation, that bananas began to reach Europe and North America in significant quantities.

The transformation of the banana into a global commodity is closely tied to the history of the Americas, particularly the rise of large-scale banana plantations in Central and South

America. In the 19th century, American entrepreneurs and companies recognized the potential profitability of bananas, which were cheap to grow and could be sold at high prices in Europe and the United States, where tropical fruits were still considered exotic luxuries.

One of the key figures in the global banana trade was Minor Keith, an American businessman who played a pivotal role in the development of banana plantations in Costa Rica and other Central American countries. Keith initially became involved in banana production through his work building railroads in Costa Rica, which were intended to facilitate the export of coffee. However, he soon realized that bananas, which grew prolifically in the tropical environment, could be an even more lucrative export crop.

Keith's success in exporting bananas to the United States helped lay the groundwork for the formation of the United Fruit Company in 1899, which would go on to dominate the global banana trade for much of the 20th century. United Fruit (now known as Chiquita Brands International) quickly established a vast network of banana plantations across Central and South America, as well as in the Caribbean. The company controlled not only the production of bananas but also the transportation and distribution networks, making it a vertically integrated business that wielded immense power over the global banana market.

The rise of banana plantations in Latin America came with significant social, political, and environmental costs. Large-scale banana production required vast amounts of land, leading to deforestation and the displacement of indigenous peoples. The workers who toiled on the plantations were often subject to harsh working conditions, low wages, and exploitation. Many of the countries that became centres of banana production, such as Honduras and Guatemala, became known as "banana republics" due to the outsized influence that foreign banana companies, particularly United Fruit, exerted over their political and economic systems.

Despite these challenges, the banana trade continued to grow throughout the 20th century, fueled by advances in transportation and refrigeration technology that made it possible to ship bananas long distances without spoilage. By the mid-1900s, bananas had become a staple fruit in many parts of the world, particularly in Europe and North America, where they were valued for their affordability, convenience, and nutritional benefits.

Today, bananas are the most traded fruit in the world, with more than 100 billion bananas consumed annually. The vast majority of bananas are produced in tropical countries, with major exporters including Ecuador, the Philippines, Costa Rica, Colombia, and Guatemala. These bananas are typically of the Cavendish variety, a monoculture that dominates global banana production due to its resistance to disease and its ability to withstand long-distance shipping.

However, the dominance of the Cavendish banana has also made the global banana industry vulnerable to disease outbreaks, particularly Panama disease, a fungal infection that has wiped out banana crops in many regions. This vulnerability highlights the challenges of monoculture farming and the need for greater diversity in banana cultivation to ensure the long-term sustainability of the fruit.

Conclusion

The history of bananas is a testament to the interconnectedness of human societies, agriculture, and global trade. From their origins in the rainforests of Southeast Asia to their spread across the ancient world and their transformation into a global commodity, bananas have played a central role in the diets, economies, and cultures of countless civilizations. Today, bananas remain one of the world's most important food crops, providing sustenance to millions of people around the globe. However, the story of the banana also raises important questions about the environmental, social, and economic costs of global food production and the challenges of sustaining a world that relies on a single variety of fruit to meet the demands of a growing population. As we look to the future, the history of bananas reminds us of the need to balance innovation with sustainability and to ensure that the fruits of our labour benefit not only consumers but also the people and ecosystems that make them possible.

Chapter 2: The Banana Empire

In the late 19th and early 20th centuries, the humble banana, a fruit previously unknown outside of its tropical regions, became a symbol of global trade, corporate power, and political manipulation. The rise of banana corporations, particularly the United Fruit Company (now Chiquita Brands International), transformed not only the global fruit market but also the economies and governments of entire countries in Latin America. The term "Banana Republic" was coined to describe nations whose political and economic systems were dominated by the interests of these fruit companies, illustrating the dangerous fusion of corporate control and political power. The Banana Empire wasn't just about producing fruit—it was about exerting influence over land, labour, and governments, often at the expense of local populations and ecosystems.

This chapter delves into the rise of these powerful banana corporations, focusing on the United Fruit Company, and examines how their control over banana production reshaped the political landscape of Central America. It also explores the dark side of the Banana Empire, including labour exploitation, environmental degradation, and the long-lasting socio-political consequences of foreign corporate dominance.

Corporate Control Over Banana Production

The Birth of the United Fruit Company

The story of the Banana Empire begins with the United Fruit Company, a corporation that came to symbolize the unchecked power of foreign business interests in Latin America. Founded in 1899 by a merger of several smaller companies, including the Boston Fruit Company, United Fruit quickly established itself as a dominant force in the global banana trade. The company's early success was driven by American businessman Minor Keith, who had previously been involved in building railroads in Costa Rica. Keith's involvement in Costa Rica's infrastructure allowed him to gain access to vast tracts of land, which he converted into banana plantations. These plantations, linked to the railroads he built, formed the backbone of United Fruit's growing empire.

United Fruit's business model was highly effective: it controlled every aspect of banana production, from the plantations where bananas were grown to the railroads and ports used to transport them to North America and Europe. This vertical integration allowed the company to minimize costs and maximize profits. The company's monopolistic control over banana production meant that it could dictate prices and production levels, putting local farmers and smaller competitors at a severe disadvantage.

As United Fruit expanded its operations across Central America, it acquired more land, often through deals with local governments that were eager for foreign investment but ill-prepared to deal with the long-term consequences of ceding control over vast agricultural regions. In exchange for building railroads, ports, and other infrastructure, United Fruit received large land concessions. In many cases, these concessions came with strings attached: the company was granted tax exemptions and other benefits, creating an unequal playing field in which local businesses and farmers struggled to compete.

By the early 20th century, United Fruit had become a corporate juggernaut, controlling not only the banana trade but also the economies of several Latin American countries. It wielded enormous influence over local governments, and its reach extended beyond the fruit market to encompass infrastructure, transportation, and even communications. For example, United Fruit was instrumental in the development of the telegraph system in Central America, which it used to coordinate its operations and maintain its grip on the region's banana industry.

Creating Monocultures and Monopolies

One of the key strategies that United Fruit employed to maintain its dominance over the banana industry was the creation of vast monoculture plantations. A monoculture is an agricultural practice in which a single crop is planted over a large area, which allows for easier management and higher yields in the short term but also creates vulnerabilities. United Fruit's decision to focus almost exclusively on the cultivation of the Cavendish banana, a variety that was prized for its durability and ease of shipping, led to the creation of banana plantations that spanned thousands of acres in countries like Honduras, Guatemala, and Costa Rica.

This practice of monoculture farming had significant ecological consequences. By clearing large swaths of tropical rainforest to make way for banana plantations, United Fruit and other companies contributed to widespread deforestation, which disrupted local ecosystems and reduced biodiversity. Additionally, the reliance on a single variety of banana made the industry highly vulnerable to disease. In the 1950s, for example, the Gros Michel banana, which had been the dominant variety for decades, was devastated by a fungal disease known as Panama disease. The company's switch to the Cavendish banana was an attempt to mitigate this problem, but the reliance on monoculture farming meant that the industry remained at risk from similar outbreaks.

United Fruit's control over land was matched by its control over labour. The company employed tens of thousands of workers across its plantations, many of whom lived in company-owned housing and were paid in company-issued currency. This system, known as the "company town" model, allowed United Fruit to maintain tight control over its workforce, who were often subjected to harsh working conditions and low wages. Labourers, many of whom were indigenous or Afro-Caribbean, had few legal protections and little recourse when it came to negotiating better pay or working conditions. Strikes and labour unrest were common, but the company frequently used its influence over local governments to suppress these movements, sometimes with violent force.

The creation of monoculture plantations and monopolistic control over the banana industry allowed United Fruit to become one of the most powerful corporations in the world. By the mid-20th century, it had cemented its place as the dominant force in the global banana trade, and its influence extended far beyond the confines of the fruit industry.

Economic and Political Domination of Banana-Producing Countries

The Birth of the "Banana Republic"

The term "Banana Republic" was coined in the early 20th century by the American writer O. Henry to describe countries in Central America whose governments were dominated by foreign banana companies, particularly United Fruit. While the term has since entered the popular lexicon as a catch-all phrase for politically unstable or corrupt nations, its original meaning was much more specific: it referred to the direct economic and political control that corporations like United Fruit exercised over entire countries.

United Fruit's economic dominance in countries like Honduras, Guatemala, and Costa Rica allowed it to exert significant influence over the governments of these nations. In many cases, local politicians were either complicit in or dependent on the company's operations, leading to a symbiotic but unequal relationship between the corporation and the state. United Fruit often acted as a state within a state, controlling vast amounts of land and infrastructure while also dictating labour policies, trade practices, and even political appointments.

One of the most notorious examples of United Fruit's political influence occurred in Guatemala in the 1950s. At the time, the country was undergoing significant political change, with the election of President Jacobo Árbenz, who sought to implement land reforms that would redistribute land to poor farmers. These reforms posed a direct threat to United Fruit, which owned vast tracts of land in Guatemala but used only a fraction of it for banana production. Árbenz's plan called for the expropriation of unused land, which would be compensated based on the declared value of the land. United Fruit, however, had long undervalued its land for tax purposes, leading to a potential conflict over compensation.

Fearing the loss of its land and influence in Guatemala, United Fruit lobbied the U.S. government to intervene. The company's connections in Washington, D.C., ran deep; several high-ranking U.S. officials, including Secretary of State John Foster Dulles and CIA Director Allen Dulles, had ties to the company. In 1954, the CIA orchestrated a coup d'état in Guatemala, ousting Árbenz and replacing him with a military regime that was more amenable to United Fruit's interests. The coup, known as Operation PBSUCCESS, marked the beginning of a decades-long period of political instability and repression in Guatemala, during which thousands of people were killed or disappeared.

This episode highlighted the extent to which United Fruit was able to leverage its economic power to influence political outcomes, not just in Latin America but also in the United States. The company's ability to shape U.S. foreign policy in Central America was a testament to its political clout, and the Guatemalan coup remains one of the most infamous examples of corporate interference in the political affairs of a sovereign nation.

The Legacy of the Banana Republics

The term "Banana Republic" may have originated in the early 20th century, but its legacy persists to this day. The economic and political domination of banana-producing countries by foreign corporations left a lasting impact on the region, shaping the development of Latin American nations in ways that are still felt today.

One of the most significant legacies of the Banana Republics was the concentration of land ownership in the hands of foreign corporations and local elites. In countries like Honduras and Guatemala, vast tracts of land were owned by a small number of wealthy landowners, leaving little room for local farmers to grow crops for themselves or for domestic markets. This concentration of land ownership exacerbated poverty and inequality in the region, as the profits from banana production flowed primarily to foreign companies and their shareholders, rather than to the local population.

The reliance on a single export crop also left these economies vulnerable to fluctuations in the global market. When demand for bananas dropped or prices fell, the economies of banana-producing countries suffered, leading to economic instability and hardship for workers. This dependence on a single commodity export—a characteristic of many Banana Republics—stifled economic diversification and hindered long-term development.

Politically, the Banana Republics were characterized by weak governance, corruption, and repression. Governments that were beholden to foreign corporations often prioritized the interests of these companies over the needs of their own citizens, leading to widespread discontent and, in some cases, violent uprisings. In Honduras, for example, the government frequently intervened on behalf of United Fruit during labour disputes, using military force to suppress strikes and protests by banana workers. These interventions often resulted in bloodshed, further entrenching the perception that the government was more interested in protecting foreign interests than in addressing the concerns of its own people.

The Banana Republics also became battlegrounds for Cold War politics, as the United States sought to prevent the spread of communism in Latin America by supporting authoritarian regimes that were friendly to American business interests. The 1954 coup in Guatemala was one of the earliest examples of U.S. intervention in the region, but it was far from the last. Throughout the 20th century, the U.S. government supported right-wing dictatorships in countries like Nicaragua, El Salvador, and Honduras, many of which had close ties to the banana industry. These regimes were often brutal, using violence and repression to maintain control and protect the interests of foreign corporations.

Labour Exploitation, Colonialism, and Environmental Destruction

The Exploitation of Banana Workers

At the heart of the Banana Empire was a system of labour exploitation that allowed companies like United Fruit to maximize their profits at the expense of local workers. The banana plantations that dotted the landscapes of Central America were built on the backs of tens of thousands of labourers, many of whom lived in abject poverty and worked in dangerous, unsanitary conditions.

Banana workers were typically paid very low wages, often in company-issued scrip rather than actual currency. This system, known as the "company town" model, meant that workers were dependent on the company for everything—from their wages to their housing to the goods they needed to buy. In many cases, workers were forced to live in company-owned housing and shop at company stores, where prices were often inflated. This created a cycle of debt and dependency, as workers struggled to make ends meet and had little recourse to improve their conditions.

Working conditions on banana plantations were harsh. Labourers worked long hours in tropical heat, often without access to clean drinking water or proper sanitation. The use of dangerous pesticides, such as DDT, was widespread, exposing workers to harmful chemicals that caused long-term health problems. Injuries were common, and workers who were hurt on the job often received little or no compensation from the company.

Attempts to organize labour unions and improve working conditions were met with fierce resistance from banana companies. United Fruit, in particular, was known for its aggressive tactics in dealing with labour unrest. The company employed a network of spies and informants to keep track of union activity and used its influence over local governments to suppress strikes and protests. In some cases, the company even resorted to violence, hiring private security forces or calling in local military units to break up strikes and intimidate workers.

One of the most infamous incidents of labour violence in the history of the Banana Empire occurred in Colombia in 1928, during what came to be known as the **Banana Massacre**. Thousands of banana workers employed by United Fruit went on strike to demand better wages and working conditions. In response, the Colombian government, under pressure from United Fruit, sent in the army to quell the strike. The soldiers opened fire on the strikers, killing an unknown number of people—estimates range from several dozen to over 1,000. The massacre was a stark reminder of the lengths to which banana companies and their government allies were willing to go to maintain control over their workforce.

Environmental Destruction and the Ecological Costs of Bananas

The environmental impact of the Banana Empire was just as devastating as its human toll. The practice of monoculture farming, which involved clearing large areas of land to plant a single crop, had far-reaching consequences for the ecosystems of Central America.

Deforestation was one of the most immediate and visible effects of banana production. In order to create space for banana plantations, vast tracts of tropical rainforest were cleared, resulting in the loss of biodiversity and the destruction of habitats for countless species of plants and animals. The loss of forest cover also contributed to soil erosion and the degradation of the land, making it less fertile over time.

The use of chemical pesticides and fertilizers on banana plantations further exacerbated environmental problems. To protect their crops from pests and diseases, banana companies relied heavily on chemicals like DDT, which were sprayed in large quantities over the plantations. These chemicals not only killed pests but also contaminated the soil and water, causing long-term damage to the environment. Pesticides used in banana farming were known to leach into nearby rivers and streams, poisoning fish and other aquatic life and affecting the health of local communities that relied on these water sources.

One of the most significant environmental challenges facing the banana industry was the spread of **Panama disease**, a fungal infection that wiped out entire plantations of the Gros Michel banana variety in the mid-20th century. The disease thrived in the monoculture conditions created by the banana plantations, and because the Gros Michel variety was so genetically uniform, there was little resistance to the disease. The devastation caused by Panama disease forced banana companies to switch to the Cavendish variety, which was more resistant to the fungus. However, the reliance on a single variety of banana left the industry vulnerable to future outbreaks, a vulnerability that persists to this day.

The environmental costs of banana production were not borne equally. While the profits from the banana trade flowed to foreign corporations and wealthy landowners, the environmental degradation caused by deforestation, pesticide use, and soil erosion was felt most acutely by the local communities who lived near the plantations. These communities often had little say in the decisions that affected their land and livelihoods, and they were left to deal with the consequences of a system that prioritized profits over sustainability.

Conclusion: The Enduring Legacy of the Banana Empire

The Banana Empire, built on the exploitation of land, labour, and resources, had far-reaching consequences for the countries of Central America and beyond. The economic and political domination of banana-producing nations by foreign corporations like United Fruit shaped the development of these countries in profound and lasting ways, contributing to inequality, instability, and environmental destruction.

The legacy of the Banana Empire is still visible today. While the influence of corporations like United Fruit has waned in recent decades, the patterns of exploitation and environmental degradation that characterized the banana industry persist. Many of the countries that were once Banana Republics continue to struggle with the effects of land concentration, poverty, and political instability, while the global banana trade remains dominated by a handful of powerful companies.

At the same time, the environmental challenges facing the banana industry have not gone away. The reliance on monoculture farming and the use of chemical pesticides continue to pose threats to both the environment and the long-term sustainability of banana production. The spread of new strains of Panama disease has raised concerns about the future of the Cavendish banana, which remains the most widely grown and consumed variety in the world.

As we reflect on the history of the Banana Empire, it is important to remember that the story of bananas is not just a story of fruit—it is a story of power, exploitation, and the complex relationships between corporations, governments, and the people who grow and consume the world's most popular fruit. The Banana Empire may have faded, but its legacy lives on in the global trade networks, labour practices, and environmental challenges that continue to shape the banana industry today.

Chapter 3: The Environmental Cost of Bananas

The global banana trade is one of the largest and most influential agricultural industries in the world, with over 100 billion bananas consumed annually. Bananas are not only a dietary staple for millions but also a crucial export crop for several tropical nations. However, behind the convenient, inexpensive fruit that lines grocery store shelves lies a significant environmental toll. Industrial banana farming, dominated by large-scale monoculture plantations, has had severe ecological consequences for the regions where bananas are grown. From deforestation to soil depletion and pesticide contamination, the environmental cost of bananas is one that has been largely hidden from consumers but remains a pressing issue for the future sustainability of the industry.

This chapter delves into the environmental impacts of banana farming, particularly focusing on the vulnerabilities of monoculture systems, the ecological damage caused by widespread deforestation and pesticide use, and the challenges of creating a more sustainable model for banana production. As we peel back the layers of industrial banana farming, it becomes clear that the convenience and affordability of the modern banana come at a high environmental price.

Monoculture Farming and Its Vulnerabilities

The Rise of Monoculture in Banana Production

Industrial banana farming is built upon the principle of monoculture—the cultivation of a single crop across vast expanses of land. While this approach allows for high yields and streamlined production processes, it also creates significant ecological vulnerabilities. Today, the global banana industry is dominated by a single variety, the Cavendish banana, which accounts for nearly all bananas sold in supermarkets worldwide.

The Cavendish banana became the dominant variety after the mid-20th century, following the widespread devastation of its predecessor, the Gros Michel banana, by Panama disease (a fungal infection). The Cavendish was chosen as a replacement because it was resistant to the strain of Panama disease that wiped out the Gros Michel. However, the decision to focus exclusively on the Cavendish had far-reaching consequences for the biodiversity of banana farming.

Monoculture farming, by its nature, reduces genetic diversity. In a typical monoculture plantation, thousands of genetically identical banana plants are grown in close proximity to one another, creating a landscape of uniformity. While this uniformity simplifies the planting, harvesting, and shipping processes, it also makes the entire crop more susceptible to pests and diseases. Because every banana plant in a monoculture plantation is genetically identical, a single pathogen or pest that can infect one plant can spread rapidly throughout the entire plantation.

The Cavendish banana is particularly vulnerable because it lacks genetic variation. While it may have been resistant to the original strain of Panama disease, new fungal pathogens have since evolved, posing an existential threat to the global banana supply. The most notable of these is Tropical Race 4 (TR4), a new strain of Panama disease that has begun to decimate Cavendish plantations in Asia, Australia, and parts of Africa. TR4 spreads through the soil, making it difficult to control once it has taken hold. As it spreads to new regions, TR4 threatens to wipe out entire banana plantations, just as the original Panama disease destroyed the Gros Michel.

The Domino Effect of Monoculture

The vulnerabilities of monoculture farming extend beyond disease susceptibility. By focusing on a single crop variety, banana plantations create an environment in which pests and diseases can thrive. Without the natural biodiversity of a multi-crop system, monocultures lack the ecological checks and balances that help control pest populations. This leads to a reliance on chemical pesticides and fertilizers, which in turn cause their own set of environmental problems (discussed later in this chapter).

Furthermore, monoculture farming depletes soil nutrients at an accelerated rate. A healthy ecosystem with diverse plant species can help maintain soil fertility by replenishing different nutrients through natural processes. However, when the same crop is grown repeatedly on the same land, the soil becomes exhausted, requiring increasingly intensive inputs of chemical fertilizers to maintain productivity. This process of soil degradation not only reduces the long-term viability of banana plantations but also contributes to erosion and the loss of arable land.

Monoculture farming also limits resilience to environmental changes. In a biodiverse farming system, different crops may respond differently to environmental stressors like drought, flooding, or temperature changes, allowing the ecosystem to adapt and recover. In a monoculture system, however, any disruption can have catastrophic consequences, as the entire crop is equally vulnerable to changing conditions. As climate change continues to affect weather patterns and growing conditions in tropical regions, the fragility of monoculture banana plantations is becoming an increasingly urgent concern.

Ecological Damage in Banana-Growing Regions

Deforestation and Habitat Loss

One of the most visible environmental impacts of banana farming is deforestation. Banana plantations, which require vast amounts of land, have been a leading cause of deforestation in tropical regions, particularly in Central and South America. Countries like Honduras, Costa Rica, and Ecuador—some of the world's largest banana producers—have experienced widespread deforestation as banana companies have cleared forests to make way for plantations.

The loss of tropical rainforest has profound ecological consequences. Tropical forests are among the most biodiverse ecosystems on the planet, home to countless species of plants, animals, and insects, many of which are found nowhere else in the world. When forests are cleared for banana plantations, the habitats of these species are destroyed, leading to a loss of biodiversity. In some cases, entire species have been driven to extinction due to deforestation caused by agricultural expansion.

The impact of deforestation extends beyond the loss of biodiversity. Tropical rainforests play a critical role in regulating the global climate by acting as carbon sinks, absorbing large amounts of carbon dioxide from the atmosphere. When forests are cut down, not only is this carbon-absorbing capacity lost, but the carbon stored in the trees is also released into the atmosphere, contributing to climate change. Deforestation in banana-growing regions thus has a double impact: it reduces biodiversity and exacerbates global warming.

Deforestation also has local environmental consequences. The removal of trees and vegetation can lead to soil erosion, particularly in regions with heavy rainfall. Without the roots of trees to hold the soil in place, rain can wash away the topsoil, reducing the fertility of the land and increasing the likelihood of landslides. This erosion can have devastating effects on both the environment and local communities, as it reduces the availability of arable land and contributes to the sedimentation of rivers and streams.

Pesticide Use and Contamination

The banana industry's reliance on monoculture farming has led to a heavy dependence on chemical pesticides to control pests and diseases. Bananas are highly susceptible to a variety of pests, including nematodes, beetles, and fungi, and in the absence of natural biodiversity, these pests can spread rapidly across plantations. To protect their crops, banana companies have turned to intensive pesticide use, often spraying chemicals over large areas.

The environmental impact of pesticide use in banana farming is severe. Pesticides not only kill pests but also harm other organisms in the ecosystem, including beneficial insects, birds, and aquatic life. The chemicals used in banana plantations frequently leach into nearby rivers, streams, and groundwater, contaminating water sources and harming aquatic ecosystems. Fish and other aquatic species are particularly vulnerable to pesticide contamination, as the chemicals disrupt their reproductive systems and can lead to population declines.

The use of pesticides also poses risks to the health of local communities and farmworkers. Many banana plantations are located near rural villages, and the chemicals sprayed on the crops can drift into residential areas, contaminating air, water, and soil. In some cases, workers on banana plantations are exposed to pesticides without adequate protective equipment, leading to long-term health problems, including respiratory issues, skin conditions, and an increased risk of cancer. The environmental justice implications of pesticide use in the banana industry are stark, as the people who bear the brunt of the health and environmental impacts are often the poorest and most marginalized.

One of the most notorious examples of pesticide-related harm in the banana industry involves the use of DBCP (dibromochloropropane), a pesticide used to control nematodes in the soil. DBCP was widely used in banana plantations in Central America during the 1960s and 1970s, despite evidence that it caused infertility in men who were exposed to it. Thousands of banana workers in countries like Nicaragua, Costa Rica, and Honduras were exposed to DBCP, and many suffered irreversible health effects as a result. The use of DBCP was eventually banned in the United States, but by that time, the damage had already been done.

Water Pollution and Soil Degradation

In addition to pesticide contamination, industrial banana farming contributes to water pollution and soil degradation in other ways. The use of chemical fertilizers, which are necessary to maintain the productivity of monoculture plantations, leads to the runoff of excess nutrients into rivers and streams. This process, known as nutrient pollution, can cause algal blooms in water bodies, depleting oxygen levels and creating "dead zones" where aquatic life cannot survive.

The degradation of soil in banana plantations is another significant environmental issue. As mentioned earlier, monoculture farming depletes soil nutrients, requiring increasingly large amounts of chemical fertilizers to sustain production. Over time, this depletes the natural fertility of the soil, making it less capable of supporting healthy plant growth. In addition to reducing the long-term viability of banana plantations, soil degradation also increases the risk of erosion, as nutrient-poor soil is more easily washed away by rain.

The environmental consequences of soil degradation are compounded by the fact that banana plantations are often located in tropical regions with fragile ecosystems. Once the soil is depleted and the land is no longer suitable for banana farming, the plantations are often abandoned, leaving behind a degraded landscape that is difficult to restore. In some cases, abandoned banana plantations are converted into cattle ranches or palm oil plantations, both of which further contribute to deforestation and environmental degradation.

The Future of Sustainable Banana Production

Given the significant environmental costs of industrial banana farming, it is clear that the current model of production is not sustainable in the long term. As demand for bananas continues to grow, the industry faces the dual challenge of meeting global demand while minimizing its environmental impact. In recent years, there have been efforts to promote more sustainable banana production practices, but these initiatives face significant obstacles.

Agroecology and Biodiversity

One of the most promising approaches to sustainable banana production is agroecology, an agricultural practice that emphasizes biodiversity, natural pest control, and soil health. Agroecological farming systems seek to replicate the diversity and complexity of natural ecosystems by planting multiple crops together and encouraging the presence of beneficial organisms that can help control pests.

In the context of banana farming, agroecological practices might involve intercropping bananas with other plants, such as beans or cassava, which can help improve soil fertility and reduce the need for chemical fertilizers. Agroforestry, which integrates trees into banana plantations, is another approach that can enhance biodiversity and improve soil health. Trees provide shade for banana plants, reduce soil erosion, and promote the retention of water and nutrients in the soil.

Agroecological approaches to banana farming are still relatively rare, as the industry has been slow to move away from the monoculture model. However, there are some examples of successful agroecological banana farms, particularly in regions where small-scale farmers are experimenting with alternative practices. These farms demonstrate that it is possible to produce bananas in a way that minimizes environmental harm while maintaining productivity.

Organic and Fair Trade Bananas

Another growing trend in the banana industry is the production of organic and Fair Trade bananas. Organic bananas are grown without the use of synthetic pesticides or fertilizers, which reduces the environmental impact of banana farming and protects the health of farmworkers and local communities. Instead of relying on chemical inputs, organic banana farmers use natural pest control methods, such as introducing beneficial insects or using organic compost to improve soil fertility.

Fair Trade certification, meanwhile, ensures that banana farmers receive a fair price for their produce and that workers on banana plantations are treated ethically. Fair Trade bananas are often grown using more sustainable practices, as the certification requires producers to meet certain environmental and social standards. By supporting organic and Fair Trade bananas, consumers can help reduce the environmental and social costs of banana production.

However, the market for organic and Fair Trade bananas is still relatively small, and these products often command a premium price. For large-scale banana producers, the transition to organic farming can be challenging, as it requires significant changes to their production systems and can result in lower yields. Additionally, the higher cost of organic and Fair Trade bananas can make them less accessible to low-income consumers, limiting their impact on the overall market.

Addressing the Threat of Panama Disease

One of the most pressing challenges facing the banana industry is the spread of Tropical Race 4 (TR4), the new strain of Panama disease that threatens to wipe out Cavendish banana plantations. The disease has already spread across much of Asia and is beginning to make inroads in Africa and Latin America, where the majority of the world's bananas are grown.

Addressing the threat of TR4 requires a multi-faceted approach. Researchers are working to develop new banana varieties that are resistant to TR4, but this is a time-consuming process, and it is unclear whether these new varieties will be able to replace the Cavendish on a large scale. In the meantime, some banana producers are experimenting with disease management techniques, such as improving soil health and using more resistant rootstocks to reduce the spread of TR4.

The long-term solution to the banana industry's vulnerability to disease may lie in moving away from monoculture farming altogether. By diversifying the types of bananas grown and encouraging greater genetic diversity, the industry can reduce its reliance on a single variety and create a more resilient production system. However, this transition will require significant changes to the way bananas are produced, marketed, and consumed.

Conclusion: The Price of Convenience

The environmental cost of bananas is a reflection of the broader challenges facing industrial agriculture. The monoculture model that has allowed for the mass production of cheap bananas has also created a system that is environmentally unsustainable and vulnerable to collapse. Deforestation, pesticide contamination, soil degradation, and the spread of diseases like Panama disease are all symptoms of a system that prioritizes short-term productivity over long-term sustainability.

As consumers, we rarely think about the environmental impact of the bananas we eat. But behind every banana lies a complex web of ecological consequences, from the destruction of tropical rainforests to the pollution of rivers and the degradation of soil. If the banana industry is to continue feeding the world's growing population, it must find ways to reduce its environmental footprint and adopt more sustainable practices.

The future of banana production will depend on the industry's ability to balance the needs of consumers with the needs of the environment. Agroecology, organic farming, and genetic diversity all offer promising paths forward, but these solutions will require a collective effort from producers, consumers, and governments. Only by rethinking the way we produce and consume bananas can we ensure that this beloved fruit remains available for generations to come, without sacrificing the health of the planet.

Part 2: Smartphones – The Digital Revolution

Chapter 4: From Sand to Silicon: Building a Smartphone

The smartphone in your pocket is more than just a sleek piece of technology; it's a product of global collabouration, involving raw materials extracted from the earth's crust, intricate engineering, and some of the most advanced manufacturing processes in human history. From the cobalt in the Democratic Republic of Congo (DRC) to the silicon chips designed in California and manufactured in Taiwan, the journey of a smartphone's components is long and complex.

In this chapter, we trace the path of a smartphone from raw materials to a finished product, exploring the origins of key materials like lithium, cobalt, and rare earth metals, the global supply chains that bring these materials together, and the intricate technical processes involved in assembling a smartphone. This journey highlights not only the incredible technological advancements that have enabled the smartphone revolution but also the environmental, ethical, and political challenges embedded in the industry.

Origins of Key Smartphone Materials

Smartphones are composed of hundreds of individual parts, many of which rely on rare and valuable materials. These materials, including lithium, cobalt, gold, tin, tantalum, and rare earth elements, are mined from various locations around the world, often in regions fraught with political instability and environmental challenges. Each of these materials plays a crucial role in the functionality of modern smartphones, enabling everything from battery life to touchscreen responsiveness.

Lithium: Powering the Battery Revolution

One of the most critical components of a smartphone is its battery, which relies on lithium-ion technology. Lithium-ion batteries are preferred for smartphones due to their high energy density, allowing devices to operate for extended periods without frequent recharging. Lithium, the lightest metal on the periodic table, is an essential material in these batteries, enabling the storage of large amounts of energy in a relatively compact form.

Lithium is primarily mined from two sources: hard rock deposits and brine pools. The largest reserves of lithium are found in the "Lithium Triangle," a region spanning parts of Chile, Bolivia, and Argentina. This area is home to some of the world's largest salt flats, where lithium is extracted from underground brine pools. These brine pools are pumped to the surface and left to evaporate, leaving behind lithium-rich salts that can be processed into lithium carbonate and lithium hydroxide, both essential for battery production.

In addition to the Lithium Triangle, Australia is also a major producer of lithium, particularly from hard rock deposits known as spodumene. These deposits are mined and processed into lithium compounds, which are then shipped to battery manufacturers around the world.

While lithium is a key enabler of modern battery technology, its extraction comes with environmental costs. The process of mining lithium from brine pools requires large amounts of water, which can deplete local water resources in arid regions like the Atacama Desert in Chile. Additionally, the chemical processes used to extract lithium can result in water contamination, affecting local ecosystems and communities.

Cobalt: The Backbone of Smartphone Batteries

Another critical material in smartphone batteries is cobalt, a metal that helps stabilize the lithium-ion battery and improve its energy density. Cobalt allows for faster charging and longer-lasting batteries, making it a vital component of modern smartphones.

Cobalt is primarily mined in the Democratic Republic of Congo (DRC), which supplies approximately 70% of the world's cobalt. The cobalt mining industry in the DRC, however, is mired in controversy. Much of the cobalt is extracted through artisanal and small-scale mining (ASM), where miners work under dangerous conditions, often using hand tools in unregulated, informal mining operations. These miners are exposed to toxic dust and have little to no protective equipment, leading to severe health risks. Child labour is also rampant in the artisanal mining sector, with children as young as seven working in the mines to supplement their families' incomes.

The DRC's cobalt mines are not only a human rights issue but also an environmental concern. The process of mining cobalt can lead to soil degradation, water pollution, and deforestation. Furthermore, the political instability in the DRC has led to corruption and conflict, with various armed groups fighting for control over the country's valuable mineral resources.

While efforts are being made to improve the transparency and ethical sourcing of cobalt through initiatives like the Responsible Cobalt Initiative (RCI), the challenge of cleaning up the supply chain remains formidable. Major tech companies are under increasing pressure to ensure that the cobalt used in their products is sourced responsibly, but the complexity of the supply chain makes this a difficult task.

Rare Earth Elements: Enabling the Smartphone Revolution

In addition to lithium and cobalt, smartphones rely on a group of materials known as rare earth elements (REEs). These elements, which include neodymium, praseodymium, dysprosium, and terbium, are essential for the production of many of the smartphone's core components, such as speakers, microphones, and vibration motors. Rare earth elements are used to create powerful magnets that drive the smartphone's haptic feedback systems and audio output.

Despite their name, rare earth elements are not particularly rare in the Earth's crust, but they are difficult to extract and process. The vast majority of the world's rare earth supply comes from China, which has dominated the market for decades. The mining and refining of rare earth elements involve environmentally damaging processes, including the use of toxic chemicals and the generation of radioactive waste.

China's near-monopoly on rare earth production has significant geopolitical implications. As smartphones and other consumer electronics continue to rely on rare earth elements, the global supply chain for these materials is increasingly vulnerable to political tensions between China and other nations. Efforts are underway to diversify the supply of rare earth elements by developing alternative mining sites in countries like Australia and the United States, but for now, China remains the dominant player in this crucial sector.

Tin, Tantalum, and Tungsten: The "3T" Conflict Minerals

Smartphones also contain significant amounts of tin, tantalum, and tungsten, collectively known as the "3T" minerals. These metals are used in a variety of smartphone components, including soldering materials (tin), capacitors (tantalum), and vibration motors (tungsten).

Many of the 3T minerals are sourced from conflict-affected regions, particularly in Central Africa. These minerals are often referred to as "conflict minerals" because their extraction and sale have been linked to armed conflict and human rights abuses. In countries like the DRC, rebel groups and militias have taken control of mining operations, using the profits to fund their activities and perpetuate violence.

In response to the ethical concerns surrounding conflict minerals, several international initiatives have been established to promote responsible sourcing. The Dodd-Frank Act in the United States, for example, requires companies to disclose whether their products contain conflict minerals sourced from the DRC or neighboring countries. Similarly, the Conflict-Free Sourcing Initiative (CFSI) provides guidelines for companies to audit their supply chains and ensure that their minerals are sourced from conflict-free regions.

However, the complexities of the global supply chain make it difficult for companies to guarantee that their products are free from conflict minerals. While progress has been made, the issue of conflict minerals remains a significant challenge for the smartphone industry.

Supply Chains in the Smartphone Industry

The journey of a smartphone from raw materials to finished product involves a vast, interconnected network of suppliers, manufacturers, and distributors. The smartphone supply chain spans multiple continents and involves thousands of companies, each playing a crucial role in the production process. From the mining of raw materials to the assembly of components, the smartphone industry relies on a highly coordinated global supply chain to deliver devices to consumers.

The Role of Suppliers

At the heart of the smartphone supply chain are the suppliers of key components, including processors, memory chips, displays, and cameras. These suppliers are responsible for manufacturing the individual parts that make up a smartphone, which are then assembled into the final product by contract manufacturers.

One of the most critical components of a smartphone is its processor, often referred to as the "brain" of the device. The leading manufacturers of smartphone processors are companies like Qualcomm, Apple, and Samsung. These companies design and manufacture the processors that power most of the world's smartphones. In particular, Apple's custom-designed A-series chips and Qualcomm's Snapdragon processors are widely regarded as some of the most powerful and efficient processors on the market.

Memory chips, which store data on the device, are another essential component of smartphones. These chips are produced by companies like Samsung, Micron, and SK Hynix. The production of memory chips involves highly specialized manufacturing processes that require clean rooms and precision engineering to ensure the chips function correctly.

Other critical components of a smartphone include the display, typically made using OLED or LCD technology, and the camera module. These components are produced by companies like LG Display, Sharp, and Sony. The displays used in modern smartphones are incredibly complex, with some high-end models incorporating flexible OLED panels that allow for features like curved screens.

Assembly and Manufacturing

Once the individual components of a smartphone have been manufactured, they are shipped to contract manufacturers for assembly. The largest and most well-known contract manufacturer in the smartphone industry is Foxconn, a Taiwanese company that assembles smartphones for major brands like Apple, Xiaomi, and Huawei. Foxconn operates massive factories in China, where millions of smartphones are assembled each year.

The assembly process involves piecing together the various components of the smartphone, including the processor, memory chips, display, and camera. Workers at Foxconn and other contract manufacturing facilities must carefully align and solder the components to create a functional device. This process requires both manual labour and automation, with robots playing an increasingly important role in the assembly line.

The final stage of the manufacturing process involves testing the smartphone to ensure that it functions correctly. This includes testing the device's performance, battery life, display quality, and camera functionality. Once the smartphone passes these tests, it is packaged and shipped to distributors around the world.

The Role of Logistics

The global supply chain for smartphones is highly reliant on efficient logistics and transportation networks. Once smartphones are assembled, they must be shipped to distribution centres, retailers, and ultimately to consumers. This involves a complex web of shipping routes, warehouses, and retail channels that span the globe.

Smartphones are typically shipped by air or sea from assembly plants in China to distribution centres in regions like North America, Europe, and Asia. From there, they are distributed to retailers and sold to consumers. The rise of e-commerce has also transformed the logistics landscape, with companies like Amazon and Alibaba playing a significant role in the distribution of smartphones.

The logistics of the smartphone industry are highly time-sensitive. Manufacturers and retailers must carefully coordinate shipments to ensure that devices are available to meet consumer demand, particularly during product launches and holiday seasons. Delays in the supply chain can result in lost sales and dissatisfied customers, making logistics a critical component of the smartphone industry.

The Technical Process of Creating a Smartphone from Raw Materials

The journey from raw materials to a fully functioning smartphone involves a series of complex technical processes, each of which plays a crucial role in the creation of the final product. These processes include the extraction and refinement of raw materials, the design and fabrication of electronic components, and the assembly and testing of the finished device.

From Sand to Silicon: The Creation of Microchips

One of the most remarkable aspects of smartphone manufacturing is the process of turning silicon, one of the most abundant elements on Earth, into the microchips that power smartphones. Silicon is found in sand and quartz, and it serves as the foundation for the semiconductors used in nearly all modern electronics.

The process of creating a microchip begins with the extraction of silicon from sand or quartz. The silicon is then purified and melted to create a high-purity silicon crystal, known as an ingot. This ingot is sliced into thin wafers, which are then processed to create the semiconductor devices that form the heart of the smartphone's processor.

The creation of a microchip involves a process known as photolithography, in which intricate patterns are etched onto the silicon wafer using ultraviolet (UV) light. These patterns define the transistors and other electronic components that make up the microchip. The transistors on a modern microchip are incredibly small, often measuring just a few nanometers in size, allowing billions of transistors to be packed onto a single chip.

Once the microchip has been fabricated, it is packaged and integrated into the smartphone's motherboard, where it serves as the central processing unit (CPU) of the device. The CPU is responsible for executing instructions, processing data, and controlling the smartphone's various functions.

Building the Display: From Liquid Crystals to OLED

The display is one of the most visible and important components of a smartphone, and its creation involves a series of technical processes that transform raw materials into the vibrant screens we interact with every day.

There are two main types of displays used in smartphones: LCD (liquid crystal display) and OLED (organic light-emitting diode). LCD displays rely on a layer of liquid crystals that are illuminated by a backlight, while OLED displays use organic compounds that emit light when an electric current is applied. OLED displays are generally preferred for high-end smartphones because they offer better contrast, more vibrant colors, and thinner form factors.

The process of creating an OLED display begins with the deposition of organic materials onto a substrate, typically made of glass or plastic. These organic materials are arranged in layers, with each layer serving a specific function, such as emitting light or transporting electrons. The layers are then patterned using photolithography to create the individual pixels that make up the display.

Once the OLED materials are in place, a layer of thin-film transistors (TFTs) is added to control the flow of electricity to each pixel. The display is then encapsulated to protect it from moisture and oxygen, which can degrade the organic materials. Finally, the display is integrated into the smartphone's body, where it is connected to the device's graphics processor and other components.

Assembling the Smartphone

The final stage of smartphone manufacturing is the assembly process, in which the various components—such as the processor, display, camera, and battery—are brought together to create a fully functioning device. This process typically takes place in large factories operated by contract manufacturers like Foxconn.

During assembly, workers carefully align and attach the components to the smartphone's motherboard. This includes soldering connections between the processor, memory chips, and other components to ensure that they communicate correctly. The battery is also installed at this stage, along with the display and camera module.

The assembly process is highly automated, with robots playing a key role in tasks like placing components on the motherboard and soldering connections. However, human workers are still needed for certain tasks, such as inspecting components for defects and performing quality control checks.

Once the smartphone is fully assembled, it undergoes a series of tests to ensure that it functions correctly. This includes testing the touchscreen, battery life, camera functionality, and overall performance. Any devices that fail these tests are sent back for repairs or rework before being packaged for shipment.

Conclusion: The Hidden Journey of Smartphones

The smartphone is a technological marvel, but its creation is far from simple. From the mining of raw materials like lithium, cobalt, and rare earth elements to the assembly of intricate components, the journey of a smartphone is a global endeavor that touches nearly every corner of the world. Along the way, the smartphone industry faces significant challenges, including ethical concerns around labour practices, environmental degradation, and geopolitical tensions.

As consumers, we rarely think about the hidden journey of the devices we use every day. Yet the story of how a smartphone is built is a reminder of the incredible complexity and interconnectedness of the modern world. Behind each smartphone lies a vast network of suppliers, manufacturers, and workers, all contributing to the creation of a device that has become indispensable to our daily lives.

In the chapters that follow, we will continue to explore the broader implications of the smartphone industry, from the environmental cost of electronic waste to the social and economic impacts of our reliance on technology. As we do, it is important to remember that the smartphone in your pocket is not just a piece of technology—it is the result of a global journey that connects us all.

Chapter 5: The Rise of the Smartphone Era

The evolution of the smartphone from a luxury gadget into a ubiquitous part of modern life is one of the most significant technological shifts of the 21st century. In just over a decade, smartphones have become indispensable tools for communication, business, entertainment, and social interaction. Once regarded as expensive, niche products, smartphones have transformed into mass-market devices that shape the way we connect with others, access information, and participate in the global economy. Today, billions of people across the world carry smartphones, giving them instant access to the internet and a wealth of applications and services.

In this chapter, we explore the rapid rise of the smartphone era, tracing its origins, the key players that drove its development, and the profound ways it has reshaped modern life. From the introduction of Apple's iPhone in 2007 to the proliferation of Android devices, we will examine how smartphones have gone from being luxury items to essential everyday tools. We will also analyze the cultural, economic, and political impact of smartphones, focusing on how they have transformed communication, information access, and business. Finally, we will look at the power dynamics between major tech companies like Apple, Samsung, and Google and the consumers who depend on their products.

The Mass Adoption of Smartphones and Its Cultural Impact

The Birth of the Modern Smartphone

Before smartphones became the all-encompassing devices we know today, mobile phones were limited in their functionality, primarily used for calls and, later, text messaging. Early attempts at creating more versatile, internet-connected devices in the 1990s and early 2000s, such as the BlackBerry and Palm Pilot, catered to business professionals rather than the general public. These devices offered basic email, internet browsing, and organizational tools, but they lacked the hardware and software sophistication that would define the modern smartphone.

The true beginning of the smartphone era came in 2007, with the release of the first-generation iPhone by Apple. While Apple was not the first company to combine a phone, internet access, and applications in a single device, the iPhone represented a revolutionary leap forward in design and user experience. With its sleek, touchscreen interface, powerful mobile operating system (iOS), and seamless integration with the internet, the iPhone set a new standard for what a mobile device could be. Its introduction marked the beginning of a seismic shift in the tech industry.

The iPhone's success was not solely due to its hardware innovations. Apple's App Store, launched in 2008, played a pivotal role in creating an ecosystem of applications that expanded the capabilities of the smartphone far beyond communication. By allowing third-party developers to create and sell apps directly to users, Apple transformed the smartphone into a platform for an endless variety of services, from gaming and social media to banking and navigation. This open market for apps helped drive the rapid adoption of smartphones and solidified their place in everyday life.

The year after the iPhone's release, Google entered the smartphone market with its Android operating system. Unlike Apple's closed system, which tightly controlled the hardware and software, Android was open-source, allowing a wide range of device manufacturers to use it. This gave companies like Samsung, HTC, and LG the opportunity to develop smartphones powered by Android, leading to a rapid expansion of the market. Android's flexibility and customization options made it the preferred choice for many consumers, and within a few years, Android overtook iOS as the dominant mobile operating system worldwide.

From Luxury to Necessity

The initial high price of smartphones positioned them as luxury items for tech enthusiasts and professionals, but their mass adoption was swift. As competition between manufacturers like Apple, Samsung, and Google intensified, the cost of smartphones began to decrease, making them more accessible to a broader demographic. By the early 2010s, smartphones were no longer seen as high-end gadgets but as essential tools for everyday life.

One of the key drivers of smartphone adoption was the proliferation of mobile internet access. As 3G and 4G networks expanded, smartphones became powerful tools for browsing the web, streaming media, and using cloud-based services. The convenience of having the internet at one's fingertips made smartphones indispensable for work, communication, and entertainment. Additionally, the integration of features like GPS, high-quality cameras, and mobile payment systems transformed smartphones into multi-functional devices that replaced a range of other technologies, from standalone cameras to credit cards.

The cultural impact of smartphones cannot be overstated. They have reshaped how we interact with the world and each other, altering social norms and behaviours. The rise of social media platforms like Facebook, Twitter, Instagram, and later, TikTok, was inextricably linked to the smartphone revolution. These platforms, optimized for mobile use, allowed users to stay connected to their friends and followers in real-time, sharing photos, videos, and updates from anywhere in the world. The ability to capture and share moments instantly has changed the way we document and experience life, blurring the lines between online and offline identities.

For younger generations, smartphones have become a primary means of social interaction. Millennials and Gen Z, in particular, are often referred to as "digital natives" because they grew up with smartphones and the internet. For them, smartphones are not just tools; they are extensions of their social lives, providing access to messaging apps, social networks, and entertainment platforms that are integral to their daily routines. The cultural shift toward constant connectivity has had both positive and negative effects, from fostering new forms of community and creativity to contributing to issues like digital addiction and the decline of face-to-face interactions.

How Smartphones Changed Communication, Business, and Information Access

The Revolution in Communication

Smartphones have radically transformed how we communicate, breaking down barriers of distance and time. Before their advent, communication options were limited to phone calls, letters, and, more recently, email and text messaging. Today, smartphones enable instant communication across multiple platforms, including video calls, social media, and messaging apps. Services like WhatsApp, iMessage, and WeChat have replaced traditional text messaging in many parts of the world, allowing users to send messages, photos, and videos instantaneously, often at no cost.

The introduction of video calling, popularized by apps like Skype and later integrated into platforms like FaceTime and Zoom, has redefined personal and professional communication. Video conferencing, once a niche tool for corporate use, became a ubiquitous part of life during the COVID-19 pandemic, enabling millions of people to work from home, attend virtual events, and stay connected with loved ones. The ability to communicate face-to-face in real-time, regardless of location, has brought a new dimension to interpersonal relationships and business communication.

Smartphones have also made communication more accessible and inclusive. For people with disabilities, smartphones offer a range of accessibility features, from voice-to-text technology to screen readers that make it easier to interact with digital content. In regions with limited access to traditional communication infrastructure, smartphones have become lifelines, enabling people to connect with the outside world through mobile networks and internet access.

The Business of Smartphones

Beyond personal communication, smartphones have had a transformative impact on the business world. Mobile technology has revolutionized the way companies operate, market their products, and interact with customers. The rise of e-commerce, driven by smartphone apps and mobile-friendly websites, has reshaped the retail landscape, allowing consumers to shop from anywhere at any time. Companies like Amazon, Alibaba, and Shopify have capitalized on this shift, creating seamless mobile shopping experiences that cater to the growing demand for convenience.

The smartphone has also democratized access to information and business tools. Entrepreneurs and small business owners now have the ability to manage their operations, process payments, and market their products directly from their phones. Mobile apps like Square and PayPal have made it possible for small vendors to accept credit card payments without the need for expensive point-of-sale systems. Social media platforms like Instagram and Facebook offer low-cost marketing opportunities, enabling businesses of all sizes to reach global audiences.

The gig economy, fueled by smartphone apps, has become a major force in the modern economy. Companies like Uber, Lyft, and DoorDash have created new job opportunities by connecting workers with customers through mobile platforms. For many, smartphones have become essential tools for earning a living, whether as drivers, delivery workers, or freelance professionals. However, the gig economy also raises important questions about labour rights and job security, as workers in these industries often lack the benefits and protections associated with traditional employment.

Information at Our Fingertips

One of the most profound changes brought about by smartphones is the way we access and consume information. With the internet in the palm of our hands, we have unprecedented access to a vast array of knowledge, from news articles and academic research to entertainment and social media content. Smartphones have transformed the way we learn, explore, and stay informed, making information more accessible than ever before.

Apps like Google, Wikipedia, and YouTube serve as digital libraries, allowing users to search for and discover information on virtually any topic. Social media platforms have become important sources of news and current events, though their role in the dissemination of information is not without controversy. The challenges of navigating a digital landscape where anyone can publish content, regardless of accuracy or credibility has led to the problems of "fake news", the rapid spread of misinformation, the prevalence of conspiracy theories and a direct threat to democracy through on-line election interference.

In addition to information access, smartphones have changed the way we interact with media. Streaming services like Spotify, Netflix, and YouTube have replaced traditional forms of media consumption, offering personalized, on-demand content that can be accessed anytime, anywhere. The smartphone's portability and versatility have made it the primary device for consuming digital content, from music and movies to news and podcasts.

The ability to access information instantly has also had a significant impact on education. Mobile learning, or "m-learning," has become a growing trend, with educational apps, online courses, and video tutorials available to anyone with a smartphone. This has democratized access to education, making it easier for people to learn new skills and acquire knowledge outside of traditional classrooms. However, it has also raised questions about the quality of digital education and the need for critical thinking in an age of information overload.

Power Dynamics Between Tech Companies and Consumers

The Influence of Apple, Samsung, and Google

The smartphone industry is dominated by a handful of major players, with Apple, Samsung, and Google leading the charge. These companies not only design and manufacture smartphones but also shape the broader technological ecosystem in which they operate. As a result, they wield significant influence over both the hardware and software that consumers rely on, as well as the data that flows through their devices.

Apple's iPhone, with its closed ecosystem of iOS apps and services, has created a loyal customer base that is deeply integrated into the company's ecosystem. From the App Store to iCloud, Apple's products and services are designed to work seamlessly together, encouraging users to remain within the Apple ecosystem. This "walled garden" approach of Apple has been highly successful, but it has also raised concerns about consumer choice and market competition. By controlling both the hardware and software of its devices, Apple has significant power over the apps and services that are available to its users, leading to accusations of anti-competitive behaviour.

Samsung, meanwhile, has carved out its own niche in the smartphone market as the largest manufacturer of Android devices. Unlike Apple, which controls every aspect of its products, Samsung relies on Google's Android operating system while differentiating itself through hardware innovation, particularly in display technology and camera quality. Samsung's dominance in the global smartphone market, particularly in regions like Asia and Europe, has made it a formidable competitor to Apple. However, like Apple, Samsung has faced criticism over issues like labour practices in its supply chain and the environmental impact of its products.

Google, as the creator of the Android operating system, plays a unique role in the smartphone industry. While Google does manufacture its own line of smartphones (the Pixel series), its primary influence comes from its control of Android, which powers the majority of the world's smartphones. Through Android, Google has access to a vast amount of user data, which it uses to drive its advertising and search businesses. This data-driven model has raised concerns about privacy and the extent to which tech companies have access to personal information.

The Data Economy and Privacy Concerns

One of the most significant power dynamics between tech companies and consumers revolves around data. Smartphones collect vast amounts of data about their users, from location and browsing history to app usage and personal preferences. This data is invaluable to tech companies, which use it to improve their products, target advertisements, and develop new services. However, the collection and use of personal data have sparked widespread concerns about privacy and surveillance.

Major tech companies like Google and Facebook have built their business models around the monetization of user data. By offering free services in exchange for access to personal information, these companies have created a data-driven economy that raises questions about consumer rights and corporate responsibility. The line between convenience and intrusion has become increasingly blurred, as consumers trade privacy for the convenience of personalized apps and services.

In recent years, there has been growing scrutiny of how tech companies handle user data, particularly in the wake of scandals like the Cambridge Analytica data breach. Governments around the world have begun to implement stricter regulations on data privacy, such as the General Data Protection Regulation (GDPR) in Europe, which gives consumers more control over their personal information. However, the sheer scale of data collection in the smartphone era makes it difficult to fully regulate or protect users from potential abuses.

The Environmental Impact of Smartphones

In addition to privacy concerns, the smartphone industry faces criticism for its environmental impact. The production of smartphones requires the extraction of rare materials, the use of energy-intensive manufacturing processes, and the generation of electronic waste (e-waste). With millions of smartphones sold each year, the environmental toll of mass production and consumption is significant.

E-waste, in particular, is a growing problem. Smartphones have relatively short lifespans, with many consumers upgrading to new models every two to three years. As a result, millions of smartphones end up in landfills, contributing to the global e-waste crisis. The toxic materials used in smartphones, such as lead and mercury, can leach into the environment, polluting soil and water.

Efforts to address the environmental impact of smartphones have included initiatives like recycling programs, modular phone designs, and the use of more sustainable materials. However, the business model of planned obsolescence, in which devices are designed to be replaced rather than repaired, remains a significant barrier to sustainability in the smartphone industry.

Conclusion: The Smartphone as a Global Force

The rise of the smartphone era has reshaped the world in ways that were unimaginable just a few decades ago. From revolutionizing communication and business to transforming the way we access information, smartphones have become an integral part of modern life. Yet, as the smartphone industry continues to evolve, it faces complex challenges related to privacy, data security, environmental sustainability, and the power dynamics between tech companies and consumers.

In the chapters to come, we will further explore the broader implications of the smartphone revolution, examining its role in global trade, technological advancement, and the future of digital society. As we navigate the smartphone era, it is crucial to understand not only the benefits but also the costs of the devices that have become such an essential part of our lives.

Chapter 6: E-Waste and the Problem of Planned Obsolescence

The rapid rise of smartphones, while a symbol of technological innovation and global connectivity, has also contributed to a growing environmental crisis: the massive and unsustainable accumulation of electronic waste, or e-waste. As consumers upgrade to new models every few years, older smartphones and other electronic devices are discarded, often ending up in landfills or being improperly recycled. This chapter delves into the environmental and ethical challenges posed by e-waste, with a particular focus on smartphones and the role of planned obsolescence—a business strategy that encourages consumers to replace devices more frequently than necessary. We will explore the implications of this practice for both consumers and the planet, while also considering potential solutions, such as recycling programs, modular phones, and ethical consumerism.

E-Waste and Its Environmental Toll

The Growing Problem of E-Waste

Electronic waste, or e-waste, is one of the fastest-growing waste streams in the world. In 2021, an estimated 57.4 million metric tons of e-waste were generated globally, and this figure is expected to increase in the coming years as more people gain access to electronic devices. Smartphones, with their relatively short lifespan and rapid replacement cycles, are a significant contributor to this problem. On average, smartphones are used for just two to three years before they are discarded or replaced, either because they become outdated or because the consumer is enticed by newer models.

The environmental impact of e-waste is severe. Discarded smartphones and other electronic devices contain toxic materials such as lead, mercury, cadmium, and brominated flame retardants, which can leach into soil and water, contaminating ecosystems and posing health risks to humans and wildlife. When e-waste is improperly disposed of—such as being burned or dumped in landfills—these toxic substances are released into the environment, contributing to air and water pollution.

Additionally, smartphones are made from valuable metals like gold, silver, copper, and rare earth elements, which are finite resources. When phones are discarded without being properly recycled, these materials are lost, leading to further environmental damage from the extraction of new resources. Mining for these metals is often environmentally destructive, involving deforestation, water pollution, and habitat destruction.

Global E-Waste Disposal

The problem of e-waste is not evenly distributed around the world. While wealthy nations like the United States, Japan, and countries in Europe are major producers of e-waste, much of it is shipped to developing countries in Africa and Asia for disposal. This practice, known as e-waste dumping, has devastating consequences for local communities.

In countries like Ghana, India, and Nigeria, informal e-waste recycling is common. Workers in these regions, often children, are tasked with extracting valuable metals from discarded electronics. Without access to proper tools or safety equipment, they are exposed to toxic chemicals and hazardous working conditions. E-waste workers frequently burn devices to extract metals, releasing harmful toxins into the air and surrounding environment. This process contaminates the soil and water, leading to long-term health problems, including respiratory issues, cancer, and neurological damage.

Despite international regulations, such as the Basel Convention, which aims to prevent the export of hazardous waste to developing countries, e-waste dumping remains widespread. The lack of enforcement mechanisms and oversight allows companies and individuals to bypass these regulations, sending large quantities of e-waste to countries with weaker environmental protections.

The environmental toll of e-waste is compounded by the fact that only a small percentage of electronic devices are properly recycled. Globally, less than 20% of e-waste is formally collected and recycled, meaning that the vast majority of discarded electronics end up in landfills or are handled by informal recycling operations. This represents a significant loss of valuable materials that could be recovered and reused in the production of new devices.

Planned Obsolescence: A Built-In Problem

The Concept of Planned Obsolescence

One of the key drivers of e-waste is planned obsolescence, a business strategy employed by tech companies to encourage consumers to upgrade to new devices more frequently. Planned obsolescence can take several forms: software updates that slow down older models, non-replaceable batteries that degrade over time, and hardware components that are designed to be difficult or impossible to repair. The result is that consumers are often forced to replace their devices long before they would naturally wear out.

The concept of planned obsolescence dates back to the early 20th century, when manufacturers in various industries began to realize that deliberately shortening the lifespan of their products could drive repeat purchases. In the tech industry, this strategy has been particularly effective. With each new smartphone model, companies market improved features such as faster processors, better cameras, and sleeker designs, making older models seem outdated and less desirable.

One of the most controversial examples of planned obsolescence in the smartphone industry came to light in 2017, when it was revealed that Apple had been deliberately slowing down older iPhone models through software updates. The company claimed that the slowdown was intended to prevent unexpected shutdowns in phones with aging batteries, but many consumers felt that the practice was designed to push them toward purchasing newer models. Apple faced significant backlash, and the incident sparked renewed scrutiny of the tech industry's approach to product longevity.

The Impact on Consumers

Planned obsolescence has significant implications for consumers, who are often left with few choices but to purchase new devices when their current ones become unusable. While smartphone manufacturers typically offer warranties and support for their products, these services are often limited, and repairs can be expensive or impractical. In many cases, it is cheaper to buy a new phone than to repair an old one, especially when key components like the battery or screen are damaged.

The lack of repairability in modern smartphones is another major issue. Most smartphones are designed with sealed batteries and glued components, making it difficult for consumers to replace parts or upgrade their devices. This design philosophy contributes to the culture of disposability that has come to define the tech industry, as consumers are encouraged to view their devices as short-term investments rather than long-lasting tools.

For consumers in low-income regions, planned obsolescence can be particularly problematic. While smartphones have become more affordable in recent years, they still represent a significant expense for many people. When a phone becomes obsolete after just a few years, it can be financially burdensome to replace it. Additionally, in regions where access to reliable internet and phone services is limited, smartphones are often the primary means of communication and access to information, making the need for long-lasting, reliable devices even more critical.

Ethical Concerns Surrounding Labour in Tech Manufacturing

The Human Cost of Smartphone Production

The ethical challenges surrounding e-waste and planned obsolescence are closely tied to the broader issue of labour exploitation in the tech manufacturing industry. The production of smartphones involves a complex global supply chain that relies on low-cost labour, often in countries with lax labour regulations. This has led to widespread concerns about worker rights, safety, and fair wages.

In many of the factories that produce smartphones and their components, workers face grueling conditions. Factories in countries like China, Vietnam, and India are known for long hours, low pay, and unsafe working environments. Employees are often required to work extensive overtime to meet production targets, and reports of worker suicides and mental health issues have raised alarm about the pressure placed on these workers.

One of the most notorious examples of labour exploitation in the smartphone industry involves Foxconn, a Taiwanese company that assembles smartphones for major brands like Apple and Samsung. In the early 2010s, a spate of suicides at Foxconn's factories in China drew attention to the harsh conditions faced by workers, many of whom lived in overcrowded dormitories and worked shifts that lasted up to 12 hours. While Foxconn and its clients have since implemented reforms, including higher wages and better working conditions, the incident highlighted the broader issue of labour exploitation in tech manufacturing.

Mining and Raw Material Extraction

In addition to factory workers, the labour practices associated with mining the raw materials used in smartphones raise significant ethical concerns. As discussed in Chapter 4, materials like cobalt and lithium are essential for smartphone batteries, but the conditions under which these materials are mined are often dangerous and exploitative.

In the Democratic Republic of Congo (DRC), where the majority of the world's cobalt is mined, many miners work in small-scale, artisanal operations with little oversight or safety measures. These miners, including children, work in hazardous conditions, using basic tools to extract cobalt from the earth. The use of child labour and the health risks associated with cobalt mining, such as respiratory problems and exposure to toxic chemicals, have drawn international criticism. Yet, despite these concerns, demand for cobalt continues to grow, driven by the need for more batteries to power smartphones and other electronics.

The extraction of rare earth elements, gold, and other materials used in smartphones also contributes to environmental degradation and labour exploitation. Mining operations in countries like China, Peru, and Brazil have been linked to deforestation, water pollution, and human rights abuses. In many cases, local communities bear the brunt of these environmental and social impacts, while the profits from mining flow to multinational corporations and foreign investors.

Potential Solutions: Recycling, Modular Phones, and Ethical Consumerism

Recycling Programs and E-Waste Management

One of the most promising solutions to the problem of e-waste is the development of more effective recycling programs. Proper recycling of smartphones can recover valuable materials like gold, silver, copper, and rare earth elements, reducing the need for new mining operations and minimizing the environmental impact of resource extraction. Additionally, recycling prevents toxic chemicals from entering the environment, reducing the risk of pollution.

Several companies and organizations have launched initiatives to improve e-waste recycling. Apple, for example, has introduced a program called "Apple Trade In," which allows consumers to return their old devices for credit toward new purchases. The company has also developed a robot called "Daisy" that is capable of disassembling iPhones and recovering key materials for reuse. Similarly, Samsung and other tech companies have implemented take-back programs that encourage consumers to recycle their old devices rather than discarding them.

However, recycling alone is not enough to address the scale of the e-waste problem. While initiatives like Apple's Daisy robot are innovative, the reality is that most smartphones are not recycled. Many consumers are unaware of recycling programs, or they lack access to convenient recycling facilities. Additionally, the recycling process itself can be inefficient, with only a small percentage of the materials in a smartphone being recovered. To make a significant impact, recycling programs need to be scaled up and made more accessible to consumers worldwide.

Modular Phones: A New Approach to Device Longevity

Another potential solution to the problem of planned obsolescence is the development of modular phones, which are designed to be easily repaired and upgraded by users. Modular phones feature components that can be swapped out or replaced individually, such as the battery, camera, or screen. This allows consumers to keep their phones for longer periods of time, as they can upgrade specific parts of the device rather than purchasing a new phone.

One of the most well-known modular phone projects is the Fairphone, a smartphone designed with sustainability and ethical labour practices in mind. Fairphone allows users to replace components like the battery, camera, and display without having to buy a new device. The company also emphasizes the use of conflict-free materials and fair labour practices in its supply chain, making it a more ethical choice for consumers.

While modular phones represent a promising alternative to planned obsolescence, they face significant challenges in gaining widespread adoption. The smartphone industry is heavily focused on sleek, compact designs, and modular phones are often bulkier and less aesthetically pleasing than their non-modular counterparts. Additionally, the cost of producing modular phones can be higher, making them less competitive in the market.

Ethical Consumerism: The Power of Choice

As awareness of the environmental and ethical challenges posed by smartphones grows, consumers are beginning to demand more responsible products. Ethical consumerism, which encourages people to consider the social and environmental impact of their purchases, has the potential to drive positive change in the tech industry. By choosing to buy from companies that prioritize sustainability and fair labour practices, consumers can help push the industry toward more ethical production models.

Several certifications and labels have emerged to guide consumers in making more responsible choices. For example, the Fairtrade certification ensures that products are made with fair labour practices and sustainable materials. While Fairtrade is more commonly associated with food products like coffee and chocolate, similar principles can be applied to electronics. The Fairphone, for instance, is an example of a device that emphasizes ethical sourcing and production.

Consumers can also reduce their environmental impact by extending the life of their devices. This can be achieved by repairing smartphones rather than replacing them, buying refurbished or second-hand devices, and supporting companies that offer longer warranties and repair services. By shifting away from the culture of disposability, consumers can help reduce e-waste and lessen the demand for new materials.

Conclusion: Rethinking Our Relationship with Technology

The rise of smartphones has brought about unprecedented convenience and connectivity, but it has also created significant environmental and ethical challenges. E-waste, labour exploitation, and the problem of planned obsolescence are deeply intertwined issues that require urgent attention from both consumers and the tech industry. As the demand for smartphones continues to grow, so too must our efforts to address the negative impacts of their production and disposal.

Solutions like improved recycling programs, modular phones, and ethical consumerism offer hope for a more sustainable and responsible future. However, meaningful change will require a concerted effort from all stakeholders, including manufacturers, governments, and consumers. By rethinking our relationship with technology and making more conscious choices, we can help reduce the environmental and human costs of the devices that have become so central to our lives.

Part 3: Gasoline – Fueling the Modern World

Chapter 7: The Discovery of Oil and the Birth of Gasoline

Oil and gasoline are the lifeblood of modern civilization. From fueling automobiles and airplanes to powering factories and generating electricity, these hydrocarbon-based fuels have driven industrial and economic growth for over a century. But their impact extends far beyond the energy they provide. The discovery of oil and the invention of gasoline reshaped global economies, transformed industries, and forever changed the course of human history. In this chapter, we explore the origins of oil extraction, the invention of gasoline, and the profound impact that both had on the rise of the automobile and modern transportation systems.

The History of Oil Extraction and Refining

Early Uses of Oil

The use of oil can be traced back thousands of years, long before it became the cornerstone of modern economies. Ancient civilizations, including the Mesopotamians, Egyptians, and Chinese, knew of the existence of crude oil, often in the form of surface seeps where oil would naturally emerge from the ground. These early societies found uses for crude oil and its byproducts in construction, medicine, and even warfare. For example, the ancient Persians and Romans used bitumen (a thick, tar-like form of crude oil) to waterproof boats and buildings. Oil was also used as a form of lighting fuel, particularly in China, where it was extracted and burned in lamps as early as the 4th century BCE.

However, it wasn't until the 19th century that oil began to be extracted and refined on a large scale. The demand for oil increased dramatically during the Industrial Revolution, driven in part by the need for lighting. Whale oil, which had been the primary source of fuel for lamps, was becoming scarce and expensive due to overhunting. This scarcity created an opportunity for an alternative, and crude oil emerged as a viable option.

The Birth of the Modern Oil Industry

The modern oil industry began in 1859, when **Edwin Drake** successfully drilled the first commercial oil well in Titusville, Pennsylvania. Drake's well struck oil at a depth of 69 feet, and his success proved that oil could be extracted from beneath the earth's surface in large quantities. This marked the beginning of the **Pennsylvania oil rush**, which brought thousands of entrepreneurs, drillers, and speculators to the region in search of black gold.

Drake's discovery set off a global quest for oil, as companies and governments recognized its potential value as a source of fuel and energy. The demand for oil was further boosted by the invention of the kerosene lamp, which provided a brighter, cleaner alternative to whale oil for lighting. Kerosene, a refined product of crude oil, became the dominant lighting fuel in the latter half of the 19th century.

The process of refining oil, which involves separating crude oil into different components through heating and distillation, was initially focused on producing kerosene. However, the refining process also produced a number of other byproducts, including gasoline. In the early days of the oil industry, gasoline was considered a waste product. It was volatile and difficult to store, and there was little demand for it. Refiners often discarded gasoline or used it as a cleaning agent.

The Global Expansion of Oil Extraction

As the 19th century progressed, oil fields were discovered in other parts of the world, leading to the rapid global expansion of the oil industry. In 1870, **John D. Rockefeller** founded the **Standard Oil Company**, which would go on to dominate the U.S. oil market and become one of the world's first multinational corporations. Through a combination of aggressive business practices, technological innovation, and control of key infrastructure,

Standard Oil became a monopoly, controlling over 90% of U.S. oil production and refining by the late 19th century.

Meanwhile, significant oil discoveries were made in countries like Russia, where the **Baku oil fields** on the Caspian Sea became the world's largest source of oil in the late 19th century. The Middle East, which would later become synonymous with oil, began to emerge as a key player in the global oil market in the early 20th century. In 1908, oil was discovered in Iran (then Persia), marking the beginning of the region's transformation into a global oil powerhouse.

The global demand for oil continued to grow, but it wasn't until the invention of the automobile and the rise of gasoline as a key fuel that oil became truly indispensable to the global economy.

The Invention of the Internal Combustion Engine and the Rise of Gasoline

The Internal Combustion Engine Revolution

The internal combustion engine is one of the most transformative inventions in history, and it played a crucial role in the rise of gasoline as a dominant fuel. While steam engines powered much of the Industrial Revolution, they were large, inefficient, and required significant amounts of coal and water to operate. The internal combustion engine, in contrast, offered a more efficient and compact way to convert fuel into mechanical energy.

The first internal combustion engines were developed in the early 19th century, but it wasn't until the late 1800s that significant progress was made. **Nikolaus Otto**, a German engineer, is credited with developing the first practical internal combustion engine in 1876. Known as the **Otto cycle engine**, it used a four-stroke process (intake, compression, combustion, and exhaust) that became the foundation for modern gasoline engines. Otto's engine ran on gasoline, which was beginning to be recognized as a valuable fuel due to its high energy content and ease of combustion.

The internal combustion engine revolutionized transportation by making it possible to create lightweight, self-powered vehicles. **Karl Benz**, another German inventor, is credited with building the first automobile powered by an internal combustion engine in 1885. Benz's vehicle, the **Motorwagen**, was the world's first practical automobile, running on gasoline and demonstrating the potential of the internal combustion engine for personal transportation.

While Benz's invention marked the beginning of the automobile era, it was **Henry Ford** who truly brought the automobile to the masses. In 1908, Ford introduced the **Model T**, a gasoline-powered car that was affordable, durable, and easy to operate. Ford revolutionized automobile production with the introduction of the assembly line, which allowed cars to be manufactured quickly and at a lower cost. The Model T became wildly popular, selling millions of units and cementing the automobile as a central feature of American life.

The rise of the automobile created an enormous demand for gasoline, transforming it from a byproduct of oil refining into one of the most valuable commodities in the world. As more people purchased cars, gasoline stations began to pop up across the United States and Europe, creating the infrastructure necessary to support a rapidly expanding network of motor vehicles.

Gasoline and the Growth of Transportation

Gasoline's dominance as a fuel was not limited to cars. The invention of the internal combustion engine also revolutionized other forms of transportation, including airplanes and ships. In 1903, the **Wright brothers** made history with the first powered flight, using a gasoline-powered engine to lift their aircraft into the air. Aviation quickly developed into a major industry, with gasoline-powered planes becoming the standard for both commercial and military aviation.

Gasoline-powered engines also found their way into marine transportation, replacing steam engines on many ships. While large ocean liners and cargo ships continued to use steam engines for several more decades, smaller vessels such as fishing boats, ferries, and private yachts began to adopt gasoline engines due to their efficiency and ease of use.

By the 1920s, gasoline had become the fuel of choice for nearly all forms of motorized transportation. The rise of the automobile, combined with innovations in aviation and marine transportation, ensured that gasoline would play a central role in shaping the 20th century.

How Gasoline Shaped Modern Transportation and Industries

The Automobile and the Transformation of Society

The widespread adoption of gasoline-powered automobiles had a profound impact on modern society, reshaping cities, industries, and lifestyles in ways that are still felt today. One of the most significant changes was the creation of car-dependent infrastructure. As more people began driving cars, governments invested heavily in the construction of roads, highways, and bridges. In the United States, the development of the **Interstate Highway System** in the 1950s and 1960s connected cities and towns across the country, making long-distance travel by car more accessible than ever before.

The rise of the automobile also contributed to the growth of suburbanization. In the post-World War II era, many families moved out of crowded urban centres and into suburban neighborhoods, which were made possible by the availability of affordable cars and the expansion of road networks. Suburbs became the hallmark of middle-class life, with gasoline-powered cars serving as the primary means of transportation between homes, workplaces, and commercial centres.

The automobile also revolutionized the economy, creating new industries and transforming existing ones. The demand for gasoline, tires, steel, and other materials necessary for car production fueled the growth of manufacturing industries around the world. In the United States, cities like Detroit became hubs of automobile production, earning the nickname "Motor City." Car manufacturers like Ford, General Motors, and Chrysler became some of the most powerful corporations in the world, driving economic growth and creating millions of jobs.

The cultural impact of the automobile was equally significant. Cars became symbols of freedom, mobility, and personal independence, particularly in countries like the United States, where driving was seen as a rite of passage. The car culture that developed in the mid-20th century, characterized by road trips, drive-in theaters, and car ownership as a status symbol, became a defining feature of modern life.

The Impact of Gasoline on Other Industries

Beyond transportation, gasoline played a critical role in powering industrial machinery and equipment. In the early 20th century, gasoline engines began to replace steam engines in factories and construction sites, leading to increased efficiency and productivity. Gasoline-powered generators and pumps allowed for the mechanization of agriculture, construction, and mining, revolutionizing industries that had previously relied on manual labour or animal power.

The oil and gasoline industry itself became a major economic force, with oil companies like **Standard Oil**, **Royal Dutch Shell**, and **British Petroleum (BP)** dominating global markets. These companies controlled not only the extraction and refining of oil but also the distribution of gasoline through their vast networks of pipelines, tankers, and gas stations.

Gasoline also found its way into consumer products beyond transportation and industry. The rise of the gasoline-powered lawnmower, for example, transformed suburban landscaping, while gasoline generators became essential for powering homes and businesses in remote areas or during power outages. Gasoline's versatility as a fuel made it indispensable across a wide range of applications.

The Environmental Consequences of Gasoline

While gasoline powered the industrial and transportation revolutions of the 20th century, it also had significant environmental consequences. The burning of gasoline in internal combustion engines releases carbon dioxide (CO_2), a greenhouse gas that contributes to global warming. As cars, planes, and ships became more prevalent, so did the emissions of CO_2 and other pollutants, leading to increased air pollution in cities and the acceleration of climate change.

The environmental impact of gasoline production extends beyond its use as a fuel. The extraction of crude oil, from which gasoline is refined, is an energy-intensive process that can lead to deforestation, habitat destruction, and oil spills. Oil spills, such as the infamous **Exxon Valdez spill** in 1989 and the **Deepwater Horizon disaster** in 2010, caused widespread environmental damage, contaminating oceans and coastal ecosystems and killing marine life.

Efforts to mitigate the environmental impact of gasoline have included the development of cleaner-burning fuels, the introduction of catalytic converters in cars to reduce emissions, and the promotion of alternative energy sources such as electric vehicles. However, the transition away from gasoline has been slow, and it remains the dominant fuel for transportation in much of the world.

Conclusion: The Birth of a New Era

The discovery of oil and the invention of gasoline were pivotal moments in the history of modern civilization. Together, they transformed transportation, reshaped industries, and fueled economic growth on a global scale. From the rise of the automobile to the expansion of global trade networks, gasoline became a symbol of progress and innovation, powering the machines that defined the 20th century.

However, the environmental and social consequences of gasoline use have also become increasingly apparent. As the world grapples with the challenges of climate change and resource depletion, the future of gasoline is uncertain. While alternative energy sources such as electric vehicles and renewable fuels offer hope for a more sustainable future, the legacy of gasoline remains deeply embedded in the fabric of modern society.

In the chapters that follow, we will explore the ongoing impact of gasoline on the global economy and environment, as well as the efforts to transition to a more sustainable energy future. As we look to the future, it is important to remember the pivotal role that gasoline has played in shaping the world we live in today.

Chapter 8: The Geopolitics of Oil

Oil, more than any other resource, has shaped the modern world in ways that extend far beyond energy production. It has redefined global trade, sparked wars, and shifted the balance of power between nations. From the rise of oil-rich states to the creation of multinational organizations like OPEC, oil has influenced geopolitics for over a century. Control over oil supplies has been central to many international conflicts, and the strategic importance of oil in global trade continues to be a driving force behind foreign policies, alliances, and power struggles.

In this chapter, we explore how oil has been both a tool and a weapon in international relations, examining its impact on the economies of oil-producing nations, its role in global conflicts, and the strategic importance of gasoline and oil in global trade. We will analyze the formation of OPEC, the various "oil wars" that have shaped international relations, and how the quest for energy security has influenced geopolitics from the 20th century to the present.

The Economic and Political Power of Oil-Producing Nations

The Rise of Oil-Rich Nations

The discovery of oil in the Middle East and other regions of the world during the early 20th century fundamentally altered the economic and political landscape of those nations lucky enough to possess vast reserves. Oil-rich countries, particularly those in the Middle East, transformed almost overnight from underdeveloped economies to some of the wealthiest nations in the world. The newfound wealth generated by oil exports allowed these countries to invest in infrastructure, education, healthcare, and military strength, and in many cases, oil revenue became the lifeblood of their economies.

Countries like Saudi Arabia, Iran, Iraq, Kuwait, and the United Arab Emirates (UAE) saw tremendous economic growth following the discovery of oil beneath their soil. Saudi Arabia, in particular, with its vast oil fields, became a dominant player in the global oil market. By the mid-20th century, it held some of the largest known reserves in the world. The Saudi royal family used its oil wealth to modernize the country, build cities, and secure the kingdom's strategic interests both regionally and internationally.

Other oil-rich nations, such as Venezuela, Russia, and Nigeria, also experienced profound economic transformations due to oil. While the distribution of oil wealth varied by country, with some governments using the resource to uplift their populations and others suffering from corruption and mismanagement, oil undeniably placed these countries on the global stage, providing them with economic leverage and political influence.

The Formation of OPEC: A Cartel to Control Oil Prices

One of the most significant developments in the geopolitics of oil was the formation of the **Organization of the Petroleum Exporting Countries (OPEC)** in 1960. OPEC was created by five founding members—Saudi Arabia, Iran, Iraq, Kuwait, and Venezuela—who sought to coordinate their oil production policies and protect their interests in the global market. The primary goal of OPEC was to ensure that oil-producing nations, rather than multinational corporations or foreign governments, would control the pricing and production of their oil.

Before OPEC, the global oil market was dominated by oil companies from the West, particularly the **"Seven Sisters"** (a group of multinational oil companies including Exxon, Chevron, and BP). These companies controlled much of the oil production and distribution in the Middle East and elsewhere, dictating prices and reaping significant profits while paying relatively little to the host nations. OPEC was established to challenge this status quo and give oil-producing countries greater control over their natural resources.

OPEC quickly grew in influence, with new members joining from the Middle East, Africa, and Latin America. By coordinating oil production and setting quotas for member countries, OPEC was able to influence global oil prices and stabilize the market in favor of its members. However, OPEC's real geopolitical power was not fully realized until the 1970s, when it flexed its economic muscle during one of the most pivotal events in oil history—the 1973 oil crisis.

The 1973 Oil Crisis: OPEC's Geopolitical Leverage

In 1973, the Arab members of OPEC, led by Saudi Arabia, used oil as a geopolitical weapon during the **Yom Kippur War**. When the United States and other Western nations supported Israel in the conflict against Egypt and Syria, Arab oil producers retaliated by imposing an oil embargo on the U.S. and its allies. The result was a dramatic reduction in oil supplies to the West, which led to skyrocketing oil prices and widespread economic disruption.

The **1973 oil crisis** marked a turning point in the geopolitics of oil. It demonstrated the power of OPEC and its ability to influence the global economy by controlling the flow of oil. The embargo caused severe fuel shortages in the U.S. and Europe, with long lines at gas stations and rationing of gasoline. The crisis also contributed to inflation and economic recessions in many Western countries.

In response, Western nations, particularly the U.S., began to reassess their dependence on foreign oil. The crisis prompted significant investment in domestic energy production, the development of strategic petroleum reserves, and a greater focus on energy conservation. It also underscored the geopolitical importance of the Middle East and the need for Western powers to maintain stable relations with oil-producing nations.

While the 1973 oil embargo lasted only a few months, its long-term impact on global politics and economics was profound. It solidified OPEC's role as a key player in the global oil market and highlighted the strategic importance of oil in international relations.

The Role of Oil in International Conflicts

Oil Wars: Conflicts Over Control of Resources

Oil has been a driving force behind numerous conflicts throughout the 20th and 21st centuries. Control over oil-rich regions has often been at the heart of international tensions, and several wars have been fought either directly or indirectly over access to oil reserves.

One of the earliest examples of oil's influence on warfare was during **World War I**, when the importance of oil became clear to military strategists. The British Royal Navy, for example, transitioned from coal-powered ships to oil-powered ships to gain a strategic advantage. Control over oil fields in the Middle East, particularly in what was then the Ottoman Empire, became a key objective for both the Allied and Central Powers.

During **World War II**, oil played an even more critical role. Germany, Japan, and the Allied powers all recognized the importance of securing reliable oil supplies to fuel their war machines. One of the main reasons behind Germany's invasion of the Soviet Union in 1941 was the desire to capture the oil-rich Caucasus region, while Japan sought control over oil fields in Southeast Asia, leading to the occupation of Indonesia (then the Dutch East Indies).

The Iran-Iraq War (1980–1988)

The **Iran-Iraq War**, one of the longest and bloodiest conflicts of the 20th century, was partly driven by disputes over oil resources and control of the strategic **Shatt al-Arab waterway**, which serves as the boundary between Iraq and Iran. Both countries, major oil producers, sought to control the waterway, which provides access to the Persian Gulf and the global oil market.

The war, which lasted from 1980 to 1988, was devastating for both sides, causing significant economic and human losses. It also disrupted oil production in the region, with attacks on oil tankers and refineries leading to fluctuations in global oil prices. The conflict drew in international powers, with the U.S., the Soviet Union, and Gulf states all providing support to one side or the other. Oil was both a cause of the conflict and a target, as both Iran and Iraq sought to weaken each other's ability to export oil and fund their war efforts.

The Gulf War (1990–1991)

Perhaps the most famous example of an oil-related conflict is the **Gulf War** of 1990–1991. In August 1990, Iraq, under the leadership of **Saddam Hussein**, invaded Kuwait, a small but oil-rich neighbor. Iraq's invasion was motivated by several factors, including economic grievances, territorial disputes, and the desire to control Kuwait's vast oil reserves.

At the time, Kuwait was one of the world's largest oil producers, and its oil wealth made it a valuable prize for Iraq, which was struggling with debt following the Iran-Iraq War. Saddam Hussein accused Kuwait of overproducing oil and driving down prices, which hurt Iraq's economy. By invading Kuwait, Iraq sought to gain control of its oil fields and increase its influence in the global oil market.

The invasion of Kuwait triggered an international crisis, with the United States and its allies condemning Iraq's actions and demanding its withdrawal. The U.S., which had significant strategic and economic interests in the Persian Gulf, led a coalition of countries in **Operation Desert Storm**, a military campaign to liberate Kuwait. After a brief but intense conflict, Iraqi forces were driven out of Kuwait, and the war ended in early 1991.

The Gulf War highlighted the strategic importance of oil in global geopolitics. The U.S. and its allies were willing to use military force to protect the flow of oil from the Persian Gulf, which was (and still is) one of the most important regions for global energy supplies. The war also underscored the vulnerability of global oil markets to political instability and conflict in the Middle East.

The Strategic Importance of Gasoline in Global Trade

Energy Security and the Global Oil Market

As the world's primary source of energy for transportation, electricity generation, and industrial production, oil has long been a cornerstone of global trade. The vast majority of the world's oil is transported by sea, with supertankers carrying crude oil from producers in the Middle East, Africa, and Latin America to consumers in North America, Europe, and Asia. The global oil market is highly interconnected, and disruptions to oil supply chains can have ripple effects across the global economy.

The strategic importance of gasoline, as a refined product of crude oil, is closely tied to the concept of **energy security**. Energy security refers to a nation's ability to access reliable and affordable energy supplies, and it has been a central concern for countries dependent on oil imports. For many industrialized nations, particularly those without significant domestic oil reserves, ensuring access to gasoline and other oil products is critical for economic stability and national security.

The need for energy security has shaped foreign policies and alliances for decades. Countries have sought to secure long-term supply agreements with oil-producing nations, invest in domestic energy production, and diversify their energy sources to reduce dependence on foreign oil. The development of **strategic petroleum reserves (SPRs)** is one way that nations have sought to mitigate the risk of supply disruptions. For example, the United States established its Strategic Petroleum Reserve in the 1970s, storing millions of barrels of oil to be used in the event of an emergency.

Chokepoints in Global Oil Trade

One of the most critical factors in the geopolitics of oil is the existence of strategic **chokepoints**—narrow waterways through which large volumes of oil must pass to reach global markets. The most famous of these chokepoints is the **Strait of Hormuz**, a narrow passage between the Persian Gulf and the Gulf of Oman. Approximately 20% of the world's oil supply passes through the Strait of Hormuz, making it one of the most strategically important waterways in the world.

The vulnerability of the Strait of Hormuz to political instability and conflict has made it a focal point of geopolitical tensions. In recent years, tensions between Iran and the United States have raised concerns about the possibility of Iran blocking the Strait in retaliation for economic sanctions or military action. Such a move could severely disrupt global oil supplies and lead to a spike in gasoline prices around the world.

Other important chokepoints in global oil trade include the **Suez Canal**, which connects the Mediterranean Sea to the Red Sea, and the **Bab el-Mandeb Strait**, which links the Red Sea to the Gulf of Aden. Both of these chokepoints are critical for oil shipments from the Middle East to Europe and North America. Disruptions in these regions, whether due to conflict or other factors, can have a significant impact on the global oil market.

The Future of Oil in Global Geopolitics

The Shift to Renewable Energy

As the world grapples with the challenge of climate change, the future of oil in global geopolitics is uncertain. The transition to renewable energy sources, such as solar, wind, and electric vehicles, has the potential to reduce global dependence on oil, particularly in the transportation sector. Many countries, including China, the European Union, and the United States, have set ambitious targets for reducing carbon emissions and increasing the use of renewable energy.

However, the shift to renewable energy is likely to be gradual, and oil will continue to play a significant role in the global economy for the foreseeable future. Even as electric vehicles become more popular, oil will still be needed for industrial processes, aviation, and petrochemical production. The pace of the energy transition will vary by region, with oil-producing nations facing unique challenges as they seek to diversify their economies and reduce their reliance on oil revenue.

Geopolitical Tensions in a Changing Energy Landscape

As the energy landscape shifts, new geopolitical tensions are likely to emerge. The transition to renewable energy could alter the balance of power between oil-producing and oil-consuming nations, with countries that invest in clean energy technologies gaining an economic and geopolitical advantage. At the same time, oil-dependent countries that fail to diversify their economies could face economic decline and political instability.

The rise of new energy technologies, such as battery storage and hydrogen fuel cells, could also create new opportunities for energy exporters and disrupt traditional energy markets. Countries with abundant renewable energy resources, such as wind and solar, could become major players in the global energy market, while those reliant on oil exports may struggle to maintain their influence.

Conclusion: Oil and Power in a Changing World

The geopolitics of oil has been a defining feature of the 20th and 21st centuries, shaping global trade, fueling conflicts, and influencing the foreign policies of nations around the world. As the world moves toward a more sustainable energy future, the role of oil in global geopolitics will continue to evolve. While the transition to renewable energy presents new challenges and opportunities, oil will remain a central factor in the balance of global power for years to come.

In the next chapter, we will explore the environmental consequences of the oil and gasoline industries, examining how the reliance on fossil fuels has contributed to climate change and what the future holds for the global energy system.

Chapter 9: The Environmental Impact of Gasoline

Gasoline has played a pivotal role in fueling industrial growth, modern transportation, and economic development for over a century. However, the environmental consequences of its widespread use have become impossible to ignore. From its contribution to climate change to its role in air pollution and ecosystem degradation, gasoline is at the heart of some of the most pressing environmental challenges of our time. This chapter explores the environmental impact of gasoline consumption, focusing on its link to greenhouse gas emissions, the degradation of air quality, and the harm it causes to ecosystems. We will also examine the efforts being made to reduce reliance on gasoline, including the rise of electric vehicles (EVs), the use of biofuels, and the transition to renewable energy.

The Link Between Gasoline and Greenhouse Gas Emissions

Gasoline as a Fossil Fuel

Gasoline is a fossil fuel, derived from crude oil, that releases carbon dioxide (CO_2) and other greenhouse gases (GHGs) when burned. These emissions contribute significantly to climate change, which is driven by the accumulation of GHGs in the Earth's atmosphere. As gasoline is combusted in vehicle engines, the carbon that was stored in crude oil for millions of years is released into the atmosphere in the form of CO_2, the most prevalent greenhouse gas. This process exacerbates the greenhouse effect, where heat from the sun is trapped in the atmosphere, leading to global warming.

The transportation sector is one of the largest sources of GHG emissions, with gasoline-powered vehicles being the primary culprits. According to the International Energy Agency (IEA), transportation is responsible for approximately 24% of global CO_2 emissions, and within that sector, road vehicles—including cars, trucks, and motorcycles—account for nearly three-quarters of emissions. The sheer number of gasoline-powered vehicles on the road worldwide, coupled with the increasing demand for personal and commercial transportation, has made gasoline a central factor in the global climate crisis.

Gasoline and the Carbon Cycle

Gasoline's impact on the carbon cycle is a major concern for environmental scientists. The combustion of gasoline adds vast amounts of CO_2 to the atmosphere, disrupting the natural balance of carbon exchange between the atmosphere, oceans, and terrestrial ecosystems. Prior to the Industrial Revolution, this balance allowed the Earth's climate to remain relatively stable. However, the burning of fossil fuels has tipped the scales, causing a sharp rise in atmospheric CO_2 concentrations. This increase in CO_2 is the leading cause of anthropogenic (human-induced) climate change, contributing to rising global temperatures, melting polar ice, and more frequent and severe weather events.

The carbon footprint of gasoline is further amplified by the energy-intensive process of extracting, refining, and transporting crude oil. From oil rigs and pipelines to refineries and distribution networks, the entire lifecycle of gasoline involves significant emissions of CO_2 and other greenhouse gases like methane (CH_4). These emissions occur at every stage of gasoline production, further worsening its environmental impact beyond what is released through combustion.

Global Warming and Climate Change

The accumulation of greenhouse gases from gasoline and other fossil fuels is directly linked to global warming and climate change. The average global temperature has increased by approximately 1.2°C since the pre-industrial era, and this warming is expected to continue unless significant reductions in GHG emissions are achieved. Climate change has wide-ranging impacts on ecosystems, weather patterns, and human societies, including rising sea levels, increased frequency of heatwaves, droughts, and intensified storms.

One of the most alarming aspects of climate change is the feedback loops it creates. For example, as polar ice melts due to rising temperatures, the reflective surface of the ice (which bounces sunlight back into space) is replaced by darker ocean water, which absorbs more heat. This accelerates the warming process, leading to further ice melt. Similarly, warming temperatures can release additional carbon from thawing permafrost or from forest ecosystems in the form of CO_2 and methane, further exacerbating climate change.

The link between gasoline consumption and climate change underscores the urgent need to transition away from fossil fuels. As global temperatures continue to rise, the environmental, economic, and social costs of inaction will become increasingly severe.

The Impact of Gasoline-Powered Vehicles on Air Quality and Public Health

Air Pollution from Gasoline Combustion

In addition to its role in climate change, gasoline-powered vehicles are major contributors to air pollution, which poses significant risks to public health and the environment. When gasoline is burned in internal combustion engines, it releases a variety of pollutants, including nitrogen oxides (NO_x), carbon monoxide (CO), volatile organic compounds (VOCs), and particulate matter (PM). These pollutants are harmful both to human health and to ecosystems, and they contribute to the formation of **ground-level ozone** (commonly known as smog), a key component of urban air pollution.

Nitrogen oxides (NO_x) are particularly problematic, as they react with VOCs in the presence of sunlight to form ozone. Ground-level ozone is a respiratory irritant that can exacerbate conditions such as asthma, bronchitis, and other lung diseases. Long-term exposure to high levels of ozone has been linked to an increased risk of cardiovascular and respiratory illnesses. Additionally, ozone can damage crops, forests, and other vegetation, reducing agricultural productivity and harming biodiversity.

Particulate matter (PM) is another dangerous byproduct of gasoline combustion, especially the fine particles (PM2.5) that can penetrate deep into the lungs and enter the bloodstream. Exposure to PM2.5 has been associated with heart attacks, strokes, lung cancer, and premature death. In urban areas with heavy traffic, high levels of particulate matter are a major concern for public health, particularly for vulnerable populations such as children, the elderly, and individuals with pre-existing health conditions.

The Global Health Burden of Air Pollution

Air pollution from gasoline-powered vehicles is a leading cause of morbidity and mortality worldwide. According to the World Health Organization (WHO), outdoor air pollution is responsible for approximately 4.2 million premature deaths each year, with transportation being a major contributor. In cities with high levels of traffic congestion, the health impacts of air pollution are particularly pronounced. Respiratory illnesses, heart disease, and lung cancer are all linked to prolonged exposure to pollutants emitted by cars, trucks, and motorcycles.

The economic costs of air pollution are also significant. In addition to the direct healthcare costs associated with treating pollution-related illnesses, air pollution reduces worker productivity, increases absenteeism, and imposes a burden on public health systems. The social and economic costs of poor air quality are especially acute in developing countries, where rapid urbanization and industrialization have led to a sharp increase in vehicle emissions, often without corresponding investments in pollution control measures.

Environmental Impact of Gasoline Emissions on Ecosystems

Gasoline emissions also take a toll on ecosystems, particularly through the deposition of air pollutants such as NO_x and sulfur dioxide (SO_2). When these pollutants combine with water vapor in the atmosphere, they form **acid rain**, which can acidify soils, lakes, and rivers. Acid rain has devastating effects on forests, aquatic life, and biodiversity. In freshwater ecosystems, for example, acidification can reduce the pH of lakes and streams, making the water too acidic for fish and other aquatic organisms to survive.

Gasoline emissions also contribute to **eutrophication**, a process in which excessive nutrient pollution (often from NO_x) leads to the overgrowth of algae in water bodies. When these algae die and decompose, they consume oxygen, creating **dead zones** where aquatic life cannot survive. Eutrophication has had a significant impact on coastal ecosystems, particularly in regions with high levels of vehicle emissions and agricultural runoff.

The environmental and public health impacts of gasoline emissions highlight the urgent need for cleaner, more sustainable alternatives to gasoline-powered transportation. The continued use of gasoline not only exacerbates climate change but also poses serious risks to human health and the environment.

Efforts to Transition Away from Gasoline

The Rise of Electric Vehicles (EVs)

One of the most promising solutions to reducing gasoline consumption and its environmental impact is the rise of **electric vehicles (EVs)**. Unlike gasoline-powered vehicles, EVs run on electricity stored in batteries, which can be generated from renewable energy sources such as solar, wind, and hydroelectric power. By eliminating the need for gasoline, EVs offer a cleaner, more sustainable alternative for personal and commercial transportation.

The adoption of electric vehicles has accelerated in recent years, driven by advancements in battery technology, government incentives, and growing consumer demand for environmentally friendly transportation options. Major automakers, including Tesla, Nissan, General Motors, and Volkswagen, have invested heavily in EV production, and many countries have set ambitious targets for phasing out gasoline-powered vehicles in favor of electric alternatives. For example, several European countries, including Norway, the Netherlands, and the United Kingdom, have announced plans to ban the sale of new gasoline and diesel cars by 2030 or 2040.

The environmental benefits of EVs are significant. Because EVs produce no tailpipe emissions, they help reduce air pollution and improve public health in urban areas. Additionally, when powered by renewable energy, EVs have a much lower carbon footprint than gasoline-powered vehicles, contributing to efforts to combat climate change.

However, the widespread adoption of EVs is not without challenges. One of the main obstacles is the environmental impact of **lithium-ion batteries**, which are used to power most electric vehicles. The mining and production of lithium, cobalt, and other materials used in EV batteries can have significant environmental and social consequences, as discussed in Chapter 4. Additionally, the disposal and recycling of EV batteries pose long-term environmental challenges.

Despite these challenges, the shift toward electric vehicles represents a major step forward in reducing the environmental impact of transportation. As battery technology continues to improve and renewable energy becomes more widely available, EVs have the potential to play a key role in the global transition away from gasoline.

Biofuels: A Renewable Alternative to Gasoline?

Biofuels offer another potential alternative to gasoline, with the promise of reducing greenhouse gas emissions and reliance on fossil fuels. Biofuels are derived from organic materials, such as plants, algae, or waste, and can be used as a substitute for or blended with traditional gasoline. Common biofuels include **ethanol**, which is made from crops like corn or sugarcane, and **biodiesel**, which is produced from vegetable oils or animal fats.

One of the primary advantages of biofuels is that they are renewable, meaning they can be produced from plants that absorb CO_2 as they grow, helping to offset the emissions generated when the fuel is burned. This creates the potential for biofuels to be "carbon neutral" or at least have lower lifecycle emissions than gasoline.

However, the environmental benefits of biofuels are far from clear and the subject of much debate. Critics argue that large-scale biofuel production can lead to deforestation, loss of biodiversity, and competition with food production. For example, the cultivation of biofuel crops like corn and soy can contribute to land-use changes and deforestation, as agricultural land is diverted from food production to fuel production. Additionally, the energy required to grow, harvest, and process biofuel crops can offset some of the emissions reductions achieved by using biofuels.

Despite these challenges, biofuels continue to be an important part of the conversation around reducing gasoline consumption. In countries like Brazil, ethanol made from sugarcane is widely used as a transportation fuel, and the development of advanced biofuels—such as those made from algae or waste materials—offers the potential for more sustainable alternatives to traditional gasoline.

The Transition to Renewable Energy

The long-term solution to reducing the environmental impact of gasoline lies in the transition to **renewable energy**. While gasoline and other fossil fuels have powered the world for over a century, the shift toward renewable energy sources like solar, wind, and hydropower is essential for addressing climate change and reducing air pollution.

Renewable energy technologies have advanced rapidly in recent years, with the cost of solar, wind power, and battery energy storage systems all falling dramatically. In many parts of the world, renewable energy is now cheaper than fossil fuels, making it a viable option for powering electric vehicles, homes, and industries. Governments and businesses are increasingly investing in renewable energy infrastructure, recognizing the need to decarbonize the global energy system. The trend is away from fuels of all types and towards electrification.

In the transportation sector, the combination of electric vehicles and renewable energy offers a pathway to a cleaner, more sustainable future. As more countries invest in EV charging infrastructure powered by renewable energy, the environmental benefits of electric transportation will continue to grow. We are already seeing the early signs of a stabilisation, and even a decline, in gasoline consumption, particularly in countries leading the EV transition such as Norway and China.

Additionally, innovations in energy storage, such as grid-scale batteries, will help ensure a stable and reliable supply of renewable energy, even when the sun isn't shining or the wind isn't blowing.

The transition to a world powered by renewable energy is not without challenges – it is a massive task. It requires significant investments in infrastructure, grid modernization, and energy storage. However, the environmental and economic benefits of a renewable energy future far outweigh the costs. By reducing reliance on gasoline and other fossil fuels, the world can mitigate the worst impacts of climate change, improve air quality, and protect ecosystems.

Conclusion: The Path to a Post-Gasoline Future

Gasoline has been a cornerstone of modern life for more than a century, fueling the cars, trucks, and planes that drive the global economy. However, its huge environmental impact, which is not just limited to carbon emissions and their effect on global warming, is now undeniable. From its contribution to climate change and air pollution to its role in ecosystem degradation, gasoline has left a profound mark on the planet, one that we now need to start erasing.

The good news is that solutions are emerging. The rise of electric vehicles, the development of biofuels, the rapidly developing technologies of batteries – particularly new chemistries such as sodium batteries - and the transition to renewable energy all offer pathways to reducing reliance on gasoline and mitigating its environmental impact. However, the transition to a post-gasoline future will require concerted efforts from governments, businesses, and individuals alike.

As we look toward the future, the challenge is clear: to build a transportation system that is cleaner, healthier, and more sustainable. The environmental costs of gasoline and it sister fossil fuels, are too high to ignore, and we need to act is now. By embracing renewable power generation, and the electrification of transport and industrial processes wherever possible, we can create a future where gasoline is no longer a driving force behind environmental destruction and massive health effects.

Part 4: The Future of Bananas, Smartphones, and Gasoline

Chapter 10: The Future of Food: Sustainable Bananas

Bananas, one of the most consumed fruits globally, have long been a symbol of both agricultural abundance and industrial exploitation. The history of banana production is marked by large-scale monoculture plantations, environmental degradation, labour exploitation, and social unrest. Today, the banana industry faces new challenges and opportunities as it seeks to create a more sustainable future. From agroecological innovations that protect against devastating diseases to fair trade practices that ensure ethical farming, the future of banana production hinges on finding solutions that balance economic, environmental, and social concerns.

This chapter explores the ongoing efforts to create a more sustainable banana industry, focusing on three key areas: diversifying banana crops to protect against diseases like Panama disease, the rise of fair trade and ethical farming models, and the role of consumers in driving change through conscious purchasing decisions. By examining these developments, we gain insight into how the banana industry can adapt to the growing demands for sustainability and ethical production while continuing to meet the global appetite for this beloved fruit.

The Vulnerability of Monocultures: Diversifying Banana Crops to Protect Against Disease

The Threat of Panama Disease and Monoculture Farming

One of the greatest challenges facing the future of banana production is the vulnerability of monoculture farming. For decades, the global banana industry has been dominated by the **Cavendish banana**, a variety prized for its durability and long shelf life, making it ideal for international trade. However, this reliance on a single variety has made the banana industry highly susceptible to disease outbreaks, particularly **Panama disease**—a soil-borne fungal pathogen that has already decimated banana plantations in several regions.

Panama disease, also known as **Fusarium wilt**, wiped out the Cavendish's predecessor, the **Gros Michel** banana, in the mid-20th century. Today, a new strain of Panama disease, known as **Tropical Race 4 (TR4)**, threatens to do the same to the Cavendish. TR4 has already spread across Asia, Australia, Africa, and parts of Latin America, leaving many banana plantations unproductive and forcing the industry to confront the urgent need for crop diversification.

The Search for Resistant Banana Varieties

To combat the threat of TR4 and other diseases, researchers and agricultural experts are working to diversify the banana crops grown around the world. One approach is the development of **disease-resistant banana varieties** that can replace or supplement the Cavendish. Scientists are using traditional breeding techniques as well as modern biotechnological tools, such as genetic modification and gene editing, to create banana varieties that are resistant to TR4 and other fungal infections.

In Uganda, for example, researchers have developed a genetically modified variety of banana that shows resistance to bacterial wilt, a major threat to banana production in East Africa. This variety could also offer hope for resistance to TR4, although the use of genetically modified organisms (GMOs) remains controversial, particularly in regions where there is public resistance to GMOs in agriculture.

Another avenue of exploration is the revival of **heirloom banana varieties** that were once common in different parts of the world but fell out of favor due to their lower yields or shorter shelf life. These bananas may not be as well-suited for international trade as the Cavendish, but they could play a crucial role in local markets and sustainable agriculture. By cultivating a wider range of banana varieties, farmers can reduce the risk of widespread disease outbreaks and increase the genetic diversity of banana crops, which is essential for long-term sustainability.

Agroecology and Sustainable Banana Farming

Agroecology, an agricultural approach that emphasizes ecological balance and biodiversity, offers another solution to the problem of monoculture farming in the banana industry. Agroecological practices promote crop diversification, soil health, and natural pest management, reducing the need for chemical inputs like pesticides and fertilizers. In banana farming, agroecology can help create more resilient ecosystems by encouraging farmers to plant a variety of crops alongside bananas, which can improve soil fertility and reduce the spread of diseases.

For example, intercropping bananas with nitrogen-fixing plants like beans or cover crops can enhance soil health, while planting trees around banana fields can provide shade and reduce water evaporation, creating a more favorable growing environment. These agroecological practices not only benefit the banana crop but also contribute to the overall sustainability of the farming system, helping to protect biodiversity and mitigate the effects of climate change.

Agroecology also emphasizes the importance of working with local ecosystems rather than imposing industrial-scale monoculture practices on the land. By fostering greater biodiversity and using traditional knowledge alongside modern scientific methods, agroecology offers a promising path for the future of banana farming, one that is more resilient to disease and environmental stresses.

Fair Trade and Ethical Farming Models: Toward a More Just Banana Industry

The Fair Trade Movement and Its Impact on Banana Production

While the environmental challenges of banana production are significant, the social and ethical issues surrounding the industry are equally important. Historically, banana plantations have been sites of labour exploitation, poor working conditions, and social inequality. In response to these injustices, the **fair trade movement** has emerged as a powerful force for change, advocating for better wages, safer working conditions, and more equitable trade relationships between farmers and consumers.

Fair trade certification ensures that banana producers—especially small-scale farmers in developing countries—receive a fair price for their fruit, which covers the cost of sustainable production and provides a stable income for farmers and their families. In addition to fair wages, fair trade standards also include provisions for worker rights, health and safety, and environmental sustainability, ensuring that banana production is both socially and environmentally responsible.

By promoting fair trade bananas, consumers can support ethical farming practices and contribute to the livelihoods of farmers in countries like Ecuador, Colombia, and Costa Rica, where much of the world's banana supply is grown. The fair trade model empowers farmers by giving them greater control over their production processes and access to global markets, helping to break the cycle of exploitation that has plagued the banana industry for decades.

Ethical Farming Beyond Fair Trade

While fair trade certification is an important step toward creating a more just banana industry, it is not the only model for ethical banana farming. Other initiatives, such as **Rainforest Alliance certification**, focus on environmental sustainability and biodiversity conservation, ensuring that bananas are grown in ways that protect tropical forests, conserve water resources, and reduce pesticide use.

Moreover, some banana producers are adopting **cooperative farming models**, where farmers pool their resources and work together to improve production techniques, share knowledge, and negotiate better prices with buyers. These cooperatives often prioritize sustainable farming practices and community development, creating a more holistic approach to banana production that benefits both the environment and local populations.

One of the key challenges facing ethical banana farming is the balance between meeting the growing global demand for bananas and maintaining sustainability. Large-scale industrial farming practices are often at odds with the principles of fair trade and environmental stewardship. However, by promoting diversified production, agroecology, and cooperative models, the banana industry can begin to shift toward a more sustainable and ethical future.

The Role of Consumers in Shaping the Future of Banana Farming

Consumer Awareness and Demand for Ethical Products

Consumers play a crucial role in shaping the future of banana farming, and their purchasing decisions can have a significant impact on the industry. As awareness of the social and environmental issues surrounding banana production grows, more consumers are seeking out **ethically sourced** and **sustainably grown** bananas. This shift in consumer behaviour has created a market for fair trade, organic, and Rainforest Alliance-certified bananas, encouraging retailers and producers to adopt more responsible practices.

In many parts of the world, supermarkets and grocery stores now offer a range of ethically certified bananas, often labeled with certifications such as **Fairtrade**, **Organic**, or **Rainforest Alliance**. These labels help consumers identify products that meet specific social and environmental standards, making it easier for them to make informed choices.

The growing demand for ethical bananas has also prompted some companies to adopt **corporate social responsibility (CSR)** initiatives, where they commit to sourcing bananas from producers who adhere to fair trade or sustainable farming practices. For example, some major retailers have pledged to sell only fair trade or Rainforest Alliance-certified bananas, creating a ripple effect throughout the supply chain that benefits farmers and the environment.

Challenges of Ethical Consumerism

Despite the positive impact of ethical consumerism, there are challenges that must be addressed to ensure the long-term sustainability of the banana industry. One of the main obstacles is the **price premium** often associated with fair trade and organic bananas. While consumers in wealthier nations may be willing to pay more for ethically sourced products, this is not always the case in lower-income regions where affordability is a top priority. As a result, the market for fair trade and organic bananas remains relatively small compared to the overall demand for conventional bananas.

Moreover, the certification process for fair trade, organic, and Rainforest Alliance products can be complex and costly, particularly for small-scale farmers who may lack the resources to meet the stringent requirements. To address this issue, some organizations are working to simplify the certification process and provide financial and technical support to farmers who want to adopt sustainable practices.

Another challenge is the **lack of transparency** in supply chains, which can make it difficult for consumers to know whether the bananas they purchase are truly ethical. While certifications like Fairtrade and Rainforest Alliance offer some level of assurance, the complexity of global supply chains means that there is always a risk of exploitation or environmental harm occurring at some stage of production.

How Consumers Can Drive Change

Despite these challenges, consumers have significant power to drive change in the banana industry. By choosing to purchase ethically sourced bananas, consumers send a message to retailers and producers that there is a market for sustainable and fair trade products. In turn, this can create incentives for producers to adopt more ethical practices and for retailers to prioritize sustainability in their sourcing decisions.

Consumers can also support the future of sustainable banana farming by advocating for greater transparency in supply chains and by holding companies accountable for their environmental and social impacts. In an age where information is more accessible than ever, consumers can use their voices to demand better practices from the companies they buy from, encouraging a shift toward more responsible banana production.

In addition to purchasing ethical products, consumers can also reduce their environmental impact by minimizing food waste. Bananas are one of the most wasted foods globally, with millions of tons of bananas discarded each year due to blemishes, ripeness, or cosmetic imperfections. By making more conscious decisions about food consumption and reducing waste, consumers can contribute to a more sustainable food system.

Conclusion: A Sustainable Future for Bananas

The future of banana farming is at a crossroads. The challenges of monoculture farming, disease outbreaks, and labour exploitation are daunting, but the growing demand for sustainable and ethical practices offers hope for a better way forward. By embracing agroecology, diversifying banana crops, and supporting fair trade and cooperative farming models, the banana industry can move toward a future that balances the needs of farmers, consumers, and the environment.

Ultimately, the future of bananas depends not only on the actions of producers and policymakers but also on the choices made by consumers. By supporting sustainable and ethically sourced bananas, consumers can play a pivotal role in shaping the industry and ensuring that the bananas we enjoy today continue to be available for generations to come. The path to sustainability is not without challenges, but with innovation, cooperation, and conscious consumerism, a more just and sustainable banana industry is within reach.

Chapter 11: The Smartphone of Tomorrow

Smartphones have transformed the way we live, work, and communicate, evolving from simple communication devices into powerful mini-computers that fit in our pockets. As we look toward the future, the next generation of smartphones promises to bring even more profound changes, driven by emerging technologies like artificial intelligence (AI), 5G networks, and quantum computing. These innovations will reshape not only the devices themselves but also the societies and economies that depend on them. However, with technological advancement comes a host of ethical and environmental challenges, from concerns about data privacy and AI ethics to the growing problem of e-waste and the digital divide.

In this chapter, we explore how future technologies will shape the next generation of smartphones and discuss the potential societal and environmental impacts of these innovations. As smartphones become even more powerful and ubiquitous, it will be essential to balance technological progress with sustainability and ethical considerations.

The Impact of Emerging Technologies on Smartphone Innovation

Artificial Intelligence (AI): Smarter, More Intuitive Devices

Artificial intelligence is already a key component of today's smartphones, powering features like voice assistants (Siri, Google Assistant), facial recognition, and predictive text. However, the role of AI in smartphones is set to expand dramatically in the coming years. The **smartphone of tomorrow** will be far more intelligent and intuitive, with AI deeply integrated into every aspect of the user experience.

Future AI-driven smartphones will likely be able to anticipate user needs and adapt to their preferences in real-time. This could include smarter personal assistants that can manage every facet of daily life, from scheduling and task management to personalized content recommendations and health monitoring. AI will also enhance features like image and speech recognition, allowing smartphones to understand and process complex tasks with greater accuracy and speed.

AI will play a significant role in **mobile security**, with advancements in biometric authentication (such as improved facial and voice recognition) making smartphones more secure. AI-powered cybersecurity tools will help protect users from malware, phishing attacks, and other cyber threats by analyzing patterns and identifying suspicious behaviour before it leads to harm.

However, the widespread integration of AI into smartphones raises important ethical questions. AI systems rely on vast amounts of data to learn and improve, raising concerns about **privacy** and **data security**. How will companies ensure that users' data is protected, and how will they prevent the misuse of AI for surveillance or other invasive purposes? As AI becomes more advanced, there will be an urgent need for transparent data practices and robust safeguards to prevent potential abuses.

5G and Beyond: Ultra-Fast Connectivity

The rollout of **5G networks** is already transforming the smartphone landscape, but the full potential of 5G is only beginning to be realized. With ultra-fast speeds, low latency, and the ability to connect millions of devices simultaneously, 5G will unlock new possibilities for smartphones, enabling richer experiences in areas like **augmented reality (AR)**, **virtual reality (VR)**, and **cloud computing**.

One of the most exciting applications of 5G is in **mobile gaming** and entertainment. 5G's low latency will make it possible to stream high-quality VR and AR experiences directly to smartphones without lag, creating immersive worlds for users to explore in real-time. This will revolutionize everything from gaming and entertainment to education and remote work.

In addition to transforming user experiences, 5G will enable **smart cities** and the **Internet of Things (IoT)** by allowing seamless communication between connected devices.

Smartphones will become central hubs for managing smart homes, controlling connected vehicles, and interacting with the physical world through AR overlays. This could lead to a more interconnected and efficient society, with smartphones facilitating everything from autonomous transportation to real-time environmental monitoring.

Looking further into the future, **6G networks** are already on the horizon, promising even faster speeds and more sophisticated use cases. While still in the early stages of development, 6G could enable technologies like **haptic communication** (the ability to transmit touch and tactile experiences) and **quantum communications**, which would revolutionize secure data transmission and real-time interaction across vast distances.

Quantum Computing: A Leap in Processing Power

While quantum computing is still in its infancy, it has the potential to revolutionize the computing capabilities of smartphones in the future. **Quantum processors**, which harness the principles of quantum mechanics to perform calculations at unprecedented speeds, could make future smartphones far more powerful than even the most advanced supercomputers of today.

Quantum computing could enable smartphones to handle complex tasks such as real-time climate modeling, genetic analysis, and cryptography with ease. It would also accelerate the development of AI, allowing for more sophisticated machine learning algorithms that can process vast amounts of data in seconds. Quantum encryption could make smartphones virtually impervious to hacking, creating a new standard for secure communications.

However, integrating quantum computing into consumer smartphones will take time. The challenges of miniaturizing quantum processors, managing qubits (the fundamental units of quantum computing), and ensuring stable, error-free calculations are immense. But as these obstacles are overcome, the future smartphone could become a powerful tool capable of solving problems that are currently beyond the reach of classical computing.

Balancing Technological Advancement with Sustainability

The Environmental Cost of Smartphone Production

While the future of smartphones promises incredible technological advancements, it is crucial to address the **environmental impact** of their production. As discussed in earlier chapters, smartphones rely on the extraction of rare materials like lithium, cobalt, and rare earth metals, which have significant environmental and social costs. The mining of these materials often leads to deforestation, water pollution, and habitat destruction, while the working conditions in many mining operations are exploitative and dangerous.

The rapid pace of smartphone innovation also exacerbates the problem of **electronic waste (e-waste)**. As new models are released each year, older devices are frequently discarded, contributing to the growing global e-waste crisis. Many of these discarded phones end up in landfills, where toxic materials like lead and mercury can leach into the soil and water, causing long-term environmental harm.

One of the key challenges for the smartphone industry is to balance **technological progress** with **sustainability**. As consumers demand more powerful and feature-rich devices, manufacturers must find ways to reduce the environmental footprint of smartphone production. This could involve the development of more **sustainable materials**, improvements in **battery technology**, and innovations in **recycling and circular economy models**.

Modular Smartphones: Extending the Lifespan of Devices

One promising approach to reducing e-waste is the development of **modular smartphones**. These phones are designed with interchangeable parts that can be easily replaced or upgraded, allowing users to extend the lifespan of their devices. Rather than discarding an entire phone when a single component (such as the battery or camera) becomes outdated, users can simply swap out the old part for a new one.

Modular smartphones have the potential to significantly reduce the environmental impact of smartphone production by minimizing the need for raw materials and reducing e-waste.

Additionally, modular designs could make it easier to recycle smartphones at the end of their life, as components can be separated and reused more efficiently.

One of the most well-known examples of a modular smartphone is the **Fairphone**, which is designed with sustainability and ethical sourcing in mind. Fairphone allows users to replace key components themselves, extending the device's lifespan and reducing its environmental footprint. While modular phones have not yet gained widespread adoption, they represent an important step toward creating a more sustainable smartphone industry.

The Role of Renewable Energy

Another critical factor in the sustainability of smartphones is the energy used to power them. As smartphones become more powerful and data-intensive, their **energy consumption** increases, both during use and in the data centres that store and process the vast amounts of information they generate. Data centres are major consumers of electricity, and unless this electricity comes from renewable sources, the environmental impact of smartphone use will continue to grow.

To mitigate this, the tech industry must transition to **renewable energy** sources like solar, wind, and hydropower. Some companies are already leading the way in this area. For example, **Apple** has committed to running its global operations on 100% renewable energy, including the data centres that power services like iCloud and the App Store. As more companies follow suit, the environmental impact of smartphone use could be significantly reduced.

Consumers also have a role to play in reducing the environmental impact of smartphones by choosing devices that are energy-efficient and supporting companies that prioritize sustainability in their operations.

Ethical Concerns: Privacy, AI, and the Digital Divide

Data Privacy and Security in the Age of AI

As smartphones become more advanced, the amount of **personal data** they collect and store will continue to grow. From location data and biometric information to browsing habits and social interactions, smartphones are repositories of vast amounts of sensitive information. This raises serious concerns about **privacy** and **data security**, particularly as AI becomes more integrated into smartphones.

AI systems rely on data to learn and improve, meaning that future smartphones will need access to even more personal information to deliver enhanced user experiences. While AI can offer significant benefits, such as personalized recommendations and improved security, the potential for misuse is high. There is a growing risk that personal data could be used for surveillance, targeted advertising, or even manipulation by malicious actors.

Ensuring **data privacy** in the age of AI will require stronger regulations and greater transparency from tech companies about how they collect, store, and use data. Users should have more control over their personal information, with the ability to opt out of data collection or limit the types of data that are shared with third parties. Additionally, advances in **encryption technologies** and **secure computing** will be essential to protecting user data from breaches and cyberattacks.

AI Ethics and the Potential for Bias

As AI plays a larger role in shaping smartphone functionality, concerns about **algorithmic bias** and **ethics** will become more pressing. AI systems are only as good as the data they are trained on, and if that data is biased or incomplete, the resulting algorithms may reinforce existing inequalities. For example, facial recognition technology has been shown to be less accurate for people with darker skin tones, leading to potential discrimination and misuse.

Ensuring that AI systems are **fair** and **inclusive** will require a concerted effort to improve the diversity of data used in training and to implement checks and balances that prevent biased outcomes. As AI becomes more embedded in smartphones, companies must take responsibility for ensuring that their algorithms do not perpetuate social inequities or violate ethical principles.

The Digital Divide: Ensuring Equal Access to Technology

While smartphones have revolutionized communication and access to information, the benefits of this technology are not evenly distributed. The **digital divide**—the gap between those who have access to modern technology and those who do not—remains a significant challenge, particularly in developing countries and low-income communities.

As smartphones become more advanced and essential to daily life, the consequences of being left behind become even more severe. Without access to smartphones and the internet, individuals and communities are excluded from economic opportunities, education, healthcare, and social services. Bridging the digital divide will require investments in infrastructure, affordable devices, and digital literacy programs to ensure that everyone can participate in the smartphone-driven world of the future.

Conclusion: Navigating the Future of Smartphones

The smartphone of tomorrow promises to be more powerful, intelligent, and interconnected than ever before. With advancements in AI, 5G, and quantum computing, the next generation of smartphones will reshape how we live, work, and communicate. However, as we move toward this exciting future, it is crucial to address the environmental, ethical, and social challenges that come with technological progress.

Creating a sustainable and equitable future for smartphones will require collabouration between tech companies, governments, and consumers. By embracing innovations in modular design, renewable energy, and ethical AI, we can ensure that the smartphones of tomorrow are not only smarter but also more sustainable and inclusive.

Chapter 12: Beyond Gasoline: The Energy Transition

For over a century, gasoline has powered the engines of industry, mobility, and economic growth. Its dominance has been intertwined with the rise of automobiles, industrialization, and global trade. However, as the environmental consequences of gasoline consumption become more severe, the world is embarking on a profound energy transition. Driven by the need to combat climate change, reduce air pollution, and ensure long-term energy security, governments, industries, and consumers are increasingly turning to renewable energy and alternative fuels. This transition marks the beginning of the end for gasoline as the world's dominant fuel, ushering in an era of electric vehicles, hydrogen power, and decarbonized energy systems.

In this chapter, we explore the major forces behind the shift away from gasoline, focusing on the role of policy and innovation in driving this transition. We will examine the rise of renewable energy alternatives such as electric vehicles (EVs) and hydrogen fuel, the policies aimed at reducing carbon emissions, and the future of transportation and global energy markets. As the world moves beyond gasoline, this transition will shape not only the future of energy but also the economic and geopolitical landscape of the 21st century.

The Role of Policy and Innovation in Reducing Reliance on Gasoline

The Need for Decarbonization

The burning of gasoline and other fossil fuels is a major contributor to **greenhouse gas emissions**, which are driving global climate change. As carbon dioxide (CO_2) levels in the atmosphere continue to rise, governments and international organizations have recognized the urgent need to **decarbonize** the global economy. The goal of decarbonization is to drastically reduce carbon emissions by transitioning from fossil fuels like gasoline to cleaner, renewable energy sources.

The consequences of climate change are already being felt in the form of rising sea levels, extreme weather events, and disruptions to ecosystems and agriculture. Without significant reductions in carbon emissions, the world is on track for even more severe climate impacts. In response, many countries have committed to ambitious targets for reducing their reliance on gasoline and other fossil fuels, with the ultimate goal of achieving **net-zero emissions** by the middle of the century.

Government Policies Driving the Energy Transition

One of the most important drivers of the energy transition is **government policy**. Around the world, national governments and international bodies are implementing a wide range of policies aimed at reducing greenhouse gas emissions and promoting the adoption of cleaner energy sources.

- **Carbon Pricing and Emissions Trading**: Many countries have introduced carbon pricing mechanisms, such as carbon taxes or **cap-and-trade** systems, to make it more expensive for companies and individuals to emit CO_2. By placing a price on carbon emissions, these policies create an economic incentive for businesses to reduce their reliance on fossil fuels and invest in cleaner technologies. Emissions trading systems, like the **European Union Emissions Trading Scheme (EU ETS)**, cap the total amount of emissions allowed and let companies buy and sell emissions permits. This encourages emissions reductions in the most cost-effective way.

- **Fuel Efficiency Standards and Emission Targets**: Governments have also introduced **fuel efficiency standards** and emissions reduction targets for the transportation sector, which accounts for a significant share of global gasoline consumption. For example, the **Corporate Average Fuel Economy (CAFE)** standards in the United States mandate improvements in fuel efficiency for cars and trucks. The **European Union** has implemented strict CO_2 emissions targets for new vehicles, encouraging automakers to produce cleaner, more fuel-efficient cars and promoting the shift toward electric vehicles.

- **Subsidies and Incentives for Clean Energy**: To accelerate the energy transition, many governments offer **subsidies** and **incentives** for the adoption of clean energy technologies. These incentives may include tax credits for purchasing electric vehicles, grants for renewable energy projects, or subsidies for research and development in energy innovation. For example, countries like Norway, the Netherlands, and Germany offer significant incentives for electric vehicle adoption, including tax exemptions, rebates, and access to special lanes and parking spaces.

- **Bans on Gasoline and Diesel Vehicles**: Several countries and cities have announced plans to **ban the sale of gasoline and diesel vehicles** in the coming decades as part of their broader decarbonization strategies. Norway, for instance, has set a target of banning the sale of new fossil fuel-powered cars by 2025, while the United Kingdom and France aim to do the same by 2030 and 2040, respectively. These bans send a clear signal to automakers and consumers that the era of gasoline is coming to an end.

Innovation and Technological Advancements

Alongside government policies, **technological innovation** is playing a crucial role in reducing the world's reliance on gasoline. Advances in battery technology, renewable energy production, and alternative fuels are making it possible to power vehicles and industries without relying on fossil fuels.

One of the most important breakthroughs in recent years has been the development of **lithium-ion batteries**, which power electric vehicles and store energy from renewable sources like solar and wind. Improvements in battery capacity, efficiency, and cost have made electric vehicles more affordable and practical for everyday use. Meanwhile, research into next-generation batteries, such as **solid-state batteries** and **lithium-sulfur batteries**, promises to further increase energy density, reduce charging times, and lower costs.

In addition to battery advancements, innovations in **hydrogen fuel cells**, **synthetic fuels**, and **energy storage technologies** are creating new possibilities for decarbonizing sectors like aviation, shipping, and heavy industry—areas where electrification is more challenging. These technologies are crucial for achieving the broader goal of transitioning away from gasoline and other fossil fuels.

Renewable Energy Alternatives: Electric Vehicles, Hydrogen, and More

The Rise of Electric Vehicles (EVs)

Electric vehicles (EVs) are at the forefront of the transition away from gasoline-powered transportation. Unlike traditional internal combustion engine (ICE) vehicles, which run on gasoline or diesel, EVs are powered by electric motors and batteries. As battery technology improves and charging infrastructure expands, EVs are becoming an increasingly viable alternative to gasoline-powered cars.

- **Advantages of EVs**: EVs offer several advantages over traditional gasoline vehicles. They produce **zero tailpipe emissions**, meaning they do not contribute to air pollution or carbon emissions during operation. EVs are also more efficient than gasoline vehicles, converting a higher percentage of energy from the grid into movement. Additionally, EVs have fewer moving parts than internal combustion engines, which means they require less maintenance and are less prone to mechanical failure.

- **Challenges and Solutions**: Despite their advantages, EVs still face several challenges that need to be addressed to ensure widespread adoption. One of the main obstacles is the **range** of electric vehicles—how far they can travel on a single charge. While range anxiety has been a concern for early EV adopters, advances in battery technology are steadily increasing the range of EVs. Models like the **Tesla Model S** and the **Lucid Air** now offer ranges of over 400 miles on a single charge, alleviating concerns about long-distance travel. Another challenge is the **charging infrastructure** needed to support a growing number of EVs on the road. Governments and private companies are investing heavily in building a network of charging stations, from fast-charging hubs along highways to residential chargers. In addition, the development of **ultra-fast chargers**, which can provide a full charge in 20–30 minutes, is making EV ownership more convenient.

- **Global Adoption of EVs**: EV adoption is accelerating globally, with sales of electric cars reaching record levels in recent years. In countries like Norway, electric vehicles now make up more than 50% of new car sales, thanks to generous government incentives and a well-developed charging network. China, the world's largest auto market, has also become a global leader in EV production and adoption, driven by government policies aimed at reducing urban air pollution and greenhouse gas emissions. Automakers are responding to this shift by investing billions of dollars in EV production. Major car manufacturers, including **General Motors**, **Volkswagen**, and **Ford**, have announced plans to phase out gasoline-powered vehicles and transition to all-electric fleets within the next decade. As more automakers commit to EVs, the global market for electric vehicles is expected to grow rapidly, further reducing the demand for gasoline.

Hydrogen: An Alternative

Hydrogen **fuel cells** have long been talked about as a promising alternative for **heavier vehicles** like trucks, buses, and ships. Hydrogen fuel cells generate electricity through a chemical reaction between hydrogen and oxygen, with the only byproduct being water vapor. This makes hydrogen fuel a **clean** and **emission-free** option for transportation and industrial applications.

- **Challenges and Solutions**: Despite its potential, hydrogen fuel faces several challenges. One of the main obstacles is the **production** of hydrogen. While hydrogen is the most abundant element in the universe, it rarely exists in its pure form on Earth and must be produced through processes like **electrolysis** (splitting water into hydrogen and oxygen) or **natural gas reforming**. Currently, nearly all hydrogen is produced using natural gas, which emits CO_2. However, **green hydrogen**—produced using renewable energy to power electrolysis—is seen as the key to unlocking hydrogen's potential as a truly clean fuel. However, the thermodynamics and economics of generating renewable electricity, using it to make hydrogen, then shipping the hydrogen, and using to make electricity again don't make much sense. Another challenge is the lack of **infrastructure** for hydrogen refueling. While electric vehicle charging stations are becoming more common, hydrogen refueling stations are still very rare. Governments and companies have been investing in expanding hydrogen infrastructure, particularly in regions like **California, Japan**, and parts of **Europe**, where hydrogen is seen as a crucial component of the energy transition and generous government subsidies have been made available. However, it does seem as if the tide is turning and many of the announced projects will not go ahead.

- **Applications of Hydrogen**: Hydrogen's potential uses extend well beyond transportation. It can be used to **store energy**, power industrial processes, and generate electricity in fuel cells. For example, hydrogen can be stored and transported as a gas or liquid, making it a flexible option for **energy storage** in grids that rely on intermittent renewable energy sources like wind and solar. Hydrogen could also play a key role in **decarbonizing industries** such as steel production, which are difficult to electrify. Despite the hype around hydrogen its viable use will be limited to a few and in transportation, even heavy goods vehicles, electrification will increasingly become the norm as battery technologies improve and costs fall.

Other Renewable Energy Alternatives: Biofuels and Synthetic Fuels

In addition to electric and hydrogen vehicles, other **renewable energy alternatives** are being developed to reduce reliance on gasoline. **Biofuels**, made from organic materials like corn, sugarcane, and algae, offer a renewable alternative to gasoline that can be used in traditional internal combustion engines. Biofuels, such as ethanol and biodiesel, are already blended with gasoline in many countries, helping to reduce carbon emissions from transportation.

Synthetic fuels, also known as **e-fuels**, are another promising alternative. These fuels are produced by combining captured CO_2 with hydrogen generated from renewable energy. Like biofuels, synthetic fuels can be used in existing internal combustion engines, making them a potential solution for decarbonizing sectors like aviation and shipping, where electrification is more difficult.

While biofuels and synthetic fuels are still in the early stages of development, they offer additional pathways for reducing gasoline consumption and transitioning to a low-carbon economy.

The Future of Transportation and the Global Energy Market

The Electrification of Transportation

The electrification of transportation is central to the energy transition, and the shift from gasoline to electric vehicles will have far-reaching effects on the global energy market. As more vehicles become electrified, demand for gasoline will decline, while demand for electricity—especially from renewable sources—will increase.

- **Integration with Renewable Energy**: One of the key advantages of electric vehicles is their potential to be powered by **renewable energy**, such as wind and solar power. As countries invest in expanding renewable energy capacity, the electrification of transportation can be seamlessly integrated into a decarbonized grid. In addition, electric vehicles can serve as mobile **energy storage** units, feeding electricity back into the grid during times of high demand (a concept known as **vehicle-to-grid** or **V2G** technology).

- **Decentralized Energy Systems**: The rise of EVs and renewable energy is also driving the development of **decentralized energy systems**, where electricity is generated and stored closer to where it is used, rather than relying on centralized power plants. Solar panels on homes, combined with EVs and home batteries, allow households to generate and store their own energy, reducing reliance on gasoline-powered transportation and fossil fuel-based electricity.

The Decline of Gasoline and the Changing Geopolitical Landscape

As the world transitions away from gasoline, the geopolitical landscape of energy will change significantly. For decades, the global economy has been shaped by the dominance of oil-rich nations and the strategic importance of fossil fuel reserves. The shift to renewable energy and alternative fuels will reduce the geopolitical influence of oil-producing countries, while countries with abundant renewable energy resources, such as solar and wind, will gain new economic and political power.

At the same time, the decline of gasoline and oil will create challenges for countries and regions that rely heavily on oil exports for their economic prosperity. These countries will need to diversify their economies and invest in new industries to remain competitive in a world that is moving beyond gasoline.

Conclusion: A World Beyond Gasoline

The transition away from gasoline is well underway, driven by a combination of technological innovation, government policies, and the urgent need to combat climate change. The rise of electric vehicles, hydrogen fuel, and renewable energy alternatives is transforming the global energy landscape, offering cleaner and more sustainable solutions for transportation and industry.

While the road to a decarbonized future is not without challenges, the momentum toward a world beyond gasoline is undeniable. As governments, industries, and consumers continue to embrace clean energy technologies, the vision of a sustainable, low-carbon future is within reach.

Conclusion: The Invisible Threads Connecting Us

In our modern world, it's easy to take for granted the everyday objects that shape our lives. Bananas, smartphones, and gasoline are all so deeply embedded in the fabric of daily existence that we often overlook the complex global systems behind them. Yet, these products—seemingly ordinary on the surface—are the result of vast, interconnected networks that span continents, cultures, and economies. Behind each banana eaten, every smartphone used, and every gallon of gasoline burned lies an intricate web of trade, labour, technology, and environmental impact.

This book has explored the stories behind bananas, smartphones, and gasoline, not merely as commodities, but as symbols of the larger forces that shape our world. These three items connect us to global supply chains that fuel economic growth, drive technological advancement, and, inevitably, place strain on the environment. As we reflect on the journey we've taken through their histories, present challenges, and futures, it becomes clear that the choices we make as consumers are deeply tied to the sustainability of our world. The invisible threads that bind us to distant farms, factories, and oil fields also tie us to a shared responsibility for shaping a more equitable and sustainable future.

The Interconnected Nature of Global Supply Chains

Bananas, smartphones, and gasoline are products of **global supply chains** that exemplify the complexity of modern trade and production systems. Each of these industries relies on resources, labour, and infrastructure spread across multiple countries, often in ways that are invisible to the end consumer. The banana that arrives on your breakfast table may have traveled thousands of miles from a plantation in Central America. The smartphone in your pocket is an assembly of components sourced from around the world—cobalt from the Democratic Republic of Congo, lithium from Chile, silicon chips from Taiwan. And the gasoline that fuels your car has its origins in oil fields that may lie under deserts in the Middle East or the plains of Texas.

What unites these seemingly disparate commodities is their **reliance on global trade** and the logistical infrastructure that makes it possible. The shipping routes, supply chains, and multinational corporations that manage the flow of bananas, smartphones, and gasoline are interconnected in ways that make the world smaller and more economically integrated. But this interconnectedness comes with significant consequences. The drive to produce these goods efficiently and at scale has led to social inequalities, environmental degradation, and a dependency on unsustainable practices.

The production of bananas, for instance, has turned much of Central America into "banana republics," where agricultural monocultures dominated by foreign corporations degrade local ecosystems and exploit labour. The smartphone industry, while fostering unprecedented connectivity and innovation, depends on rare minerals that are often mined under harsh and exploitative conditions. Gasoline, which powered the industrial revolution and transformed economies, is now at the centre of the global climate crisis, its combustion contributing to rising greenhouse gas emissions.

As these supply chains grow more complex, they become harder to manage sustainably. Yet, as consumers, we are often unaware of the environmental and ethical tolls embedded in the products we use. The invisibility of these global systems makes it easy to ignore the far-reaching impacts of our consumption, even as our demand for bananas, smartphones, and gasoline drives these industries forward.

The Potential for Change Through Informed Consumption

Despite the challenges posed by the global systems behind bananas, smartphones, and gasoline, there is **significant potential for change**. The decisions consumers make—whether at the grocery store, when upgrading their phone, or when filling up their car—can collectively shape the future of global trade, technology, and sustainability. The key to unlocking this potential lies in **informed consumption**, where individuals understand the origins of the products they buy and the broader consequences of their purchasing choices.

Consumer awareness is already beginning to drive change in some industries. In the banana sector, the growing demand for **Fair Trade** and **organic** bananas reflects a shift toward more sustainable and ethical production methods. Fair Trade certification ensures that banana farmers receive a fair price for their crops, while also promoting environmental stewardship and community development. This is a model that could expand across other agricultural sectors, encouraging more responsible practices that protect both people and the planet.

Similarly, in the smartphone industry, there is increasing interest in ethically sourced materials and sustainable manufacturing practices. Companies like **Fairphone** are leading the way by designing modular phones that can be easily repaired or upgraded, reducing electronic waste. Ethical sourcing of conflict-free minerals is another area where consumers can make a difference by supporting companies that prioritize transparency and social responsibility in their supply chains. As more consumers demand sustainable and ethical products, companies will be incentivized to shift their practices to meet these expectations.

The transition away from gasoline-powered vehicles toward **electric vehicles (EVs)** is perhaps one of the most visible examples of how consumer behaviour can drive meaningful environmental change. As governments promote policies that support the adoption of EVs and renewable energy, consumers are increasingly making the choice to invest in cleaner alternatives. The rise of electric cars, coupled with advancements in battery technology, promises to reduce the carbon footprint of transportation—a sector that has long been reliant on gasoline and fossil fuels.

But informed consumption is not just about choosing the right products; it's also about **advocating for systemic change**. Consumers have the power to influence governments and corporations by demanding better regulations, sustainable practices, and transparency in supply chains. By supporting policies that promote decarbonization, fair labour practices, and environmental protection, consumers can help ensure that the systems producing bananas, smartphones, and gasoline evolve in ways that prioritize sustainability and ethical responsibility.

Final Thoughts on the Future of Global Trade and Environmental Responsibility

As we look to the future, the challenges and opportunities facing the industries that produce bananas, smartphones, and gasoline highlight the broader dilemmas of **global trade** and **environmental responsibility**. The systems that sustain our modern way of life are, at their core, unsustainable in their current form. The intensive agricultural practices that produce bananas degrade ecosystems, monoculture farming depletes biodiversity, and the industry's reliance on global supply chains increases carbon emissions. Smartphones, while remarkable technological achievements, are entwined in extractive practices that exploit both natural resources and labour. Gasoline, the cornerstone of 20th-century growth, is now a key driver of climate change, threatening the future of the planet.

To navigate the path forward, we must **reimagine global trade** to align with the principles of **sustainability** and **equity**. This requires a concerted effort from all stakeholders—governments, corporations, and consumers—to rethink how goods are produced, distributed, and consumed.

On a global scale, governments must take the lead in enacting policies that regulate industries, ensure fair trade, and promote environmental sustainability. For instance, international agreements that limit greenhouse gas emissions, support sustainable agricultural practices, and protect workers' rights are essential for mitigating the negative impacts of global trade. Meanwhile, corporations must commit to ethical sourcing, transparency in their supply chains, and investment in sustainable technologies.

Technological innovation will play a key role in this transformation. The future of smartphones lies in **circular economies**, where products are designed for durability, repairability, and recyclability. Renewable energy will replace gasoline as the primary source of power for transportation, with **electric vehicles** and **hydrogen fuel cells** leading the way. Meanwhile, advances in **agroecology** and **genetic research** offer the potential to create more resilient, disease-resistant banana crops that reduce the environmental footprint of large-scale agriculture.

Yet, at the heart of this transition lies the role of **individual consumers**. Our choices matter—whether it's the banana we pick off the shelf, the phone we choose to buy, or the car we drive. These choices, multiplied by millions of people, can drive global systems toward a more sustainable future. By supporting fair trade products, reducing electronic waste, and choosing cleaner energy sources, consumers hold the power to reshape industries and create a more equitable and sustainable world.

The invisible threads connecting bananas, smartphones, and gasoline reveal the intricate dependencies that bind us to each other and to the planet. As we continue to benefit from the fruits of global trade and technological progress, we must also recognize our shared responsibility to ensure that these systems are sustainable, ethical, and just. The future is in our hands, and the decisions we make today will determine the world we leave for future generations.

Glossary of Terms: Bananas, Smart Phones, and Gasoline

A

- **Agroecology**: A sustainable farming approach that integrates ecological principles with agricultural production, emphasizing biodiversity, soil health, and environmentally friendly practices.

- **AI (Artificial Intelligence)**: The simulation of human intelligence by machines, particularly computer systems, which includes learning, reasoning, problem-solving, and adaptation. AI is increasingly used in smartphones for voice assistants, predictive algorithms, and personalized user experiences.

- **Android**: An open-source mobile operating system developed by Google, widely used in smartphones and tablets. It allows various manufacturers to customize the system for their devices.

- **Assembly Line**: A production method where a product is assembled in a step-by-step manner by multiple workers or machines. Pioneered by Henry Ford, this technique revolutionized industries, including the automobile sector.

B

- **Banana Republic**: A derogatory term historically used to describe politically unstable countries in Latin America whose economies are heavily dependent on the export of bananas and dominated by foreign corporations.

- **Biofuels**: Renewable energy sources derived from organic materials such as plant matter (corn, sugarcane) or animal fats. Biofuels like ethanol and biodiesel are used as alternatives to gasoline and diesel.

- **Biodiversity**: The variety of plant, animal, and microorganism species in a particular habitat or ecosystem. In agriculture, higher biodiversity often leads to more resilient and sustainable ecosystems.

C

- **Cavendish Banana**: The most widely consumed banana variety in the world, known for its long shelf life and resilience in transportation. It dominates global banana trade but is vulnerable to diseases like Panama disease.

- **Circular Economy**: An economic model focused on minimizing waste and maximizing resource use by designing products for durability, reuse, repair, and recycling.

- **Climate Change**: Long-term changes in temperature, precipitation, and other atmospheric conditions caused by natural factors and human activities, primarily the burning of fossil fuels like gasoline.

- **Conflict Minerals**: Natural resources, such as cobalt or tin, that are mined in conditions of armed conflict and human rights abuses, particularly in regions like the Democratic Republic of Congo.

D

- **Decarbonization**: The process of reducing or eliminating carbon dioxide emissions from economic activities, particularly through the transition from fossil fuels to renewable energy sources.

- **Digital Divide**: The gap between individuals and communities that have access to modern information and communication technology (ICT), such as smartphones and the internet, and those who do not.

- **Diversification (in agriculture)**: The practice of growing multiple types of crops on the same land to reduce dependency on a single crop and enhance resilience to pests, diseases, and climate change.

E

- **E-Waste**: Discarded electronic devices, including smartphones, computers, and appliances, that often end up in landfills. E-waste poses environmental and health risks due to the toxic substances they contain.

- **Electric Vehicle (EV)**: A vehicle powered by electricity, typically stored in batteries, rather than gasoline. EVs are seen as a cleaner alternative to traditional internal combustion engine vehicles.

- **Emissions Trading System (ETS)**: A market-based approach to controlling pollution by providing economic incentives for reducing emissions. Governments set a cap on emissions, and companies can buy and sell allowances based on their emission levels.

F

- **Fair Trade**: A certification and movement that ensures producers in developing countries receive fair prices and work under good conditions, while also promoting sustainable environmental practices.

- **Fossil Fuels**: Natural resources like coal, oil, and natural gas formed from the remains of ancient plants and animals. These fuels are burned for energy but contribute significantly to global warming and environmental degradation.

- **Fuel Efficiency Standards**: Government regulations that set the minimum fuel economy requirements for vehicles, encouraging manufacturers to produce more fuel-efficient and less polluting cars.

G

- **Gasoline**: A liquid fossil fuel derived from crude oil, used primarily to power internal combustion engines in vehicles. Gasoline is a significant source of greenhouse gas emissions.

- **Global Supply Chain**: The interconnected network of producers, suppliers, manufacturers, and distributors that collabourate across countries to produce and deliver goods like bananas, smartphones, and gasoline.

- **Greenhouse Gas Emissions (GHG)**: Gases like carbon dioxide (CO_2), methane (CH_4), and nitrous oxide (N_2O) that trap heat in the Earth's atmosphere, contributing to global warming and climate change.

H

- **Hydrogen Fuel Cell**: A device that generates electricity through a chemical reaction between hydrogen and oxygen, producing only water as a byproduct. Hydrogen fuel cells are seen as a clean alternative for transportation and energy storage.

I

- **Internal Combustion Engine (ICE)**: An engine that generates power by burning gasoline, diesel, or other fuels. ICEs have powered most of the world's transportation for over a century but are gradually being replaced by electric alternatives.

- **Internet of Things (IoT)**: The network of interconnected devices, vehicles, and appliances that can communicate with each other through the internet, often controlled via smartphones.

L

- **Lithium-Ion Battery**: A rechargeable battery commonly used in smartphones, electric vehicles, and other electronics. It has high energy density and is key to powering modern devices, but its production involves resource-intensive mining.

M

- **Monoculture**: The agricultural practice of growing a single crop species over a large area. Monocultures, such as the widespread cultivation of Cavendish bananas, are vulnerable to disease and pests, leading to environmental risks.

- **Modular Smartphone**: A smartphone designed with interchangeable components, allowing users to repair or upgrade individual parts (such as the camera or battery) rather than replacing the entire device. Modular designs promote sustainability by reducing e-waste.

N

- **Net-Zero Emissions**: Achieving a balance between the amount of greenhouse gases emitted and the amount removed from the atmosphere. This goal is essential for addressing climate change and is often targeted for mid-century by many countries and companies.

O

- **OPEC (Organization of the Petroleum Exporting Countries)**: A group of oil-producing nations that coordinates the production and pricing of oil to stabilize the global oil market. OPEC members include countries in the Middle East, Africa, and Latin America.

P

- **Panama Disease (TR4)**: A devastating fungal disease that affects banana plants, particularly the Cavendish variety. The spread of Tropical Race 4 (TR4) has threatened global banana production, highlighting the risks of monoculture farming.

- **Planned Obsolescence**: A business strategy where products are designed to have a limited lifespan, encouraging consumers to replace them more frequently. This is often cited in the smartphone industry and contributes to e-waste.

R

- **Renewable Energy**: Energy sources that are naturally replenished, such as solar, wind, and hydropower. Renewable energy is essential for reducing reliance on fossil fuels like gasoline and lowering carbon emissions.

S

- **Silicon**: A chemical element used as the primary material for semiconductors in electronics, including smartphones. Silicon chips are essential for the functioning of modern computing devices.

- **Strategic Petroleum Reserve (SPR)**: A country's stockpile of petroleum, maintained for emergency use to mitigate the effects of disruptions in oil supply. The U.S. maintains one of the largest SPRs in the world.

- **Supply Chain Transparency**: The practice of ensuring that companies' supply chains are visible and traceable, allowing for ethical oversight of labour practices and environmental impacts.

T

- **Tech Monopoly**: Large technology companies, such as Apple and Google, that dominate markets by controlling hardware, software, and distribution channels. These companies exert significant influence over consumer behaviour and innovation.

V

- **Vehicle-to-Grid (V2G)**: A technology that allows electric vehicles to communicate with and feed energy back into the power grid, helping balance supply and demand for electricity.

Z

- **Zero-Emission Vehicle (ZEV)**: A vehicle that produces no tailpipe emissions, such as electric cars or hydrogen fuel cell vehicles. ZEVs are central to efforts to reduce air pollution and combat climate change.

This glossary encapsulates key terms that reflect the underlying themes of interconnectedness, sustainability, and the global systems behind the production and consumption of bananas, smartphones, and gasoline. These terms provide a framework for understanding the complex dynamics shaping the past, present, and future of global trade and environmental responsibility.

Resources for Further Reading: Bananas, Smart Phones, and Gasoline

On Bananas and Global Agriculture:

- **Koeppel, Dan.** *Banana: The Fate of the Fruit That Changed the World.* (2008) This book delves into the history of the banana, tracing its journey from Southeast Asia to its dominance in global markets. It covers the socio-political impacts of banana plantations and explores the looming threat of diseases like Panama disease.

- **Striffler, Steve, and Moberg, Mark (Eds.).** *Banana Wars: Power, Production, and History in the Americas.* (2003) A collection of essays examining the historical and political dynamics of banana production in Latin America, with particular focus on labour conditions, U.S. intervention, and the role of multinational corporations.

- **Johnston, Jake, and Lawrence, S. Adam.** *The High Cost of Cheap Bananas: How Chiquita, Dole, and Del Monte Built a Banana Empire.* (2010) A detailed report on the environmental and labour practices in the banana industry, particularly focusing on the role of major corporations in Central America.

- **Fair Trade International.** *Fair Bananas: Fairtrade Standards for Banana Production.* A guide to Fairtrade standards for banana production, offering insights into ethical farming practices and the economic benefits of fair trade for producers and labourers.

On Smartphones, Technology, and Supply Chains:

- **Goldstein, Paul.** *Taming the Sun: Innovations to Harness Solar Energy and Power the Planet.* (2018) A look into the renewable energy revolution, with insights into how advances in technology, including smartphones, are key to the future of energy storage and clean energy deployment.

- **Parikka, Jussi.** *A Geology of Media.* (2015) This book investigates the material basis of digital technologies, tracing how minerals, metals, and resources from around the world power our modern devices, including smartphones.

- **Duhigg, Charles, and Bradsher, Keith.** "How the U.S. Lost Out on iPhone Work." *The New York Times.* (2012) An article that explores Apple's global supply chain, focusing on the economic and labour conditions in China, where iPhones are produced.

- **Minter, Adam.** *Junkyard Planet: Travels in the Billion-Dollar Trash Trade.* (2013) An exploration of global waste and recycling markets, offering insights into the fate of discarded smartphones and the challenges posed by electronic waste (e-waste).

- **Fairphone.** *The Story Behind Your Phone: A Look at the Ethical and Sustainable Approach of Fairphone.* A report by Fairphone, a company known for its sustainable and ethical smartphone production practices, offering insights into the future of responsible electronics manufacturing.

On Gasoline, Energy Transition, and the Future of Transportation:

- **Yergin, Daniel.** *The Prize: The Epic Quest for Oil, Money, and Power.* (1991) A Pulitzer Prize-winning history of the global oil industry, examining how gasoline and petroleum have shaped global geopolitics, economies, and conflicts.

- **Lovins, Amory B.** *Reinventing Fire: Bold Business Solutions for the New Energy Era.* (2011) This book provides a roadmap for transitioning away from fossil fuels, including gasoline, focusing on renewable energy, energy efficiency, and the role of technological innovation.

- **Smil, Vaclav.** *Energy: A Beginner's Guide.* (2006) A comprehensive overview of the role energy has played in shaping human society, from the use of gasoline and fossil fuels to the future of renewable energy.

- **Shellenberger, Michael.** *Apocalypse Never: Why Environmental Alarmism Hurts Us All.* (2020) A critical look at environmental movements, including discussions about the transition from gasoline to renewable energy. Shellenberger argues for a more nuanced approach to energy policy and environmental responsibility.

- **IEA (International Energy Agency).** *Global EV Outlook 2023: Scaling Up the Transition to Electric Mobility.* The IEA's annual report provides key insights into the growth of electric vehicles (EVs), the infrastructure needed to support them, and how the shift from gasoline to electricity is transforming transportation systems.

On Global Supply Chains and Trade:

- **Baldwin, Richard.** *The Great Convergence: Information Technology and the New Globalization.* (2016) This book explores how globalization has evolved in the digital age, highlighting the role of global supply chains in industries like smartphones, agriculture, and energy.

- **Milanovic, Branko.** *Global Inequality: A New Approach for the Age of Globalization.* (2016) An analysis of how global trade and supply chains, including those that produce bananas, smartphones, and gasoline, have contributed to rising inequality and economic disparity around the world.

- **Schor, Juliet.** *Plenitude: The New Economics of True Wealth.* (2010) A book that challenges conventional economic growth models, advocating for sustainable consumption patterns and mindful trade practices, particularly relevant in industries like agriculture and electronics.

- **Friedman, Thomas L.** *The World is Flat: A Brief History of the Twenty-First Century.* (2005) This best-seller examines globalization and the interconnectedness of economies, with a focus on how technology, including smartphones, has flattened the world by linking distant economies and cultures.

On Sustainability and Environmental Responsibility:

- **Steffen, Will, et al.** *The Anthropocene: Are Humans Now Overwhelming the Great Forces of Nature?* (2007) A scientific examination of humanity's impact on the Earth's systems, including the environmental consequences of gasoline consumption and industrial agriculture.

- **McKibben, Bill.** *Falter: Has the Human Game Begun to Play Itself Out?* (2019) In this urgent call to action, McKibben discusses the environmental impacts of fossil fuels like gasoline and the need for a rapid transition to renewable energy in the face of climate change.

- **Crutzen, Paul J. and Stoermer, Eugene F.** *The Anthropocene: The Human Impact on Earth's Ecosystems.* An academic exploration of the Anthropocene—the geological age defined by human influence on the planet, focusing on the consequences of industrial farming, fossil fuel use, and technological waste.

- **Raworth, Kate.** *Doughnut Economics: Seven Ways to Think Like a 21st-Century Economist.* (2017) A framework for rethinking global economic systems, focusing on sustainability and how we can transition toward a balance between ecological and social well-being.

- **Jackson, Tim.** *Prosperity Without Growth: Foundations for the Economy of Tomorrow.* (2017) This book critiques the traditional focus on economic growth and explores how societies can achieve prosperity through sustainable practices, addressing both the environmental and economic challenges linked to global trade and consumption.

Index for Bananas, Smart Phones, and Gasoline

Agroecology, 25, 28, 81, 106, 118
air pollution, 61, 71, 73, 74, 75, 77, 78, 93, 96, 97, 111
Android, 39, 40, 45, 106, 118
Apple, 33, 34, 39, 40, 44, 45, 50, 52, 53, 90, 111, 113, 118
artificial intelligence, 86, 124
assembly line, 34, 59

banana republics, 3, 9, 102
battery technology, 30, 75, 76, 89, 95, 96, 103
Biodiversity, 25, 107, 118
Biofuels, 76, 98, 106, 118
biometric authentication, 87

carbon footprint, 72, 75, 103
Carbon Pricing, 94, 118
Cavendish banana, 10, 13, 19, 20, 21, 27, 80
circular economy, 89
climate change, 4, 5, 22, 23, 61, 62, 69, 70, 71, 72, 73, 75, 77, 78, 81, 93, 94, 100, 104, 107, 109, 110, 111, 115, 125, 126
cobalt, 1, 3, 29, 30, 31, 37, 52, 75, 89, 101, 107
Conflict Minerals, 32, 107, 118
corporate social responsibility, 83

Data Economy, 45, 119
data privacy, 46, 86, 91
decarbonization, 93, 95, 103
deforestation, 3, 9, 13, 18, 20, 22, 23, 25, 31, 49, 52, 62, 76, 89
digital divide, 86, 92

electric vehicles, 4, 62, 69, 71, 75, 76, 77, 78, 93, 95, 96, 97, 99, 100, 103, 104, 109, 111, 114
Emissions Trading, 94, 108, 119
energy security, 63, 67, 68, 93, 122, 125, 126
energy storage, 77, 96, 98, 99, 109, 113
environmental impact, 3, 17, 23, 25, 26, 27, 45, 46, 48, 53, 54, 62, 71, 72, 75, 76, 77, 78, 85, 89, 90, 101, 122
ethical consumerism, 48, 55, 84
ethical labour practices, 54

E-waste, 46, 49, 55, 108

fair trade, 79, 82, 83, 84, 85, 104, 105, 113
fossil fuels, 2, 4, 70, 72, 73, 76, 77, 78, 93, 94, 95, 96, 103, 107, 111, 114, 115, 125
Fuel Efficiency Standards, 94, 108, 119

global supply chains, 3, 29, 84, 101, 104, 114
greenhouse gas emissions, 71, 76, 93, 94, 97, 102, 104, 108, 122

hydrogen fuel cells, 69, 96, 104

Internal Combustion Engine, 58, 109, 120

Lithium-ion batteries, 30

Modular Smartphones, 89, 120
monoculture, 2, 10, 12, 13, 17, 18, 19, 20, 21, 22, 23, 24, 26, 27, 79, 80, 81, 85, 104, 110

net-zero emissions, 94

OPEC, 63, 64, 65, 110, 120

Panama disease, 10, 13, 18, 19, 20, 21, 26, 27, 79, 80, 107, 112
planned obsolescence, 4, 46, 48, 50, 51, 53, 54, 55

recycling, 46, 48, 49, 50, 53, 55, 76, 89, 107, 113
renewable energy, 4, 69, 70, 71, 75, 76, 77, 78, 90, 92, 93, 94, 95, 98, 99, 100, 103, 107, 113, 114, 115, 122, 125

silicon, 29, 35, 101
Supply Chain Transparency, 111, 121

transportation, 8, 9, 12, 34, 56, 59, 60, 61, 62, 67, 69, 71, 74, 75, 76, 77, 78, 88, 93, 94, 96, 97, 98, 99, 100, 103, 104, 107, 109, 114

vehicle-to-grid, 99

wind and solar power, 99

This index is organized to reflect the key topics and concepts covered in the book *Bananas, Smart Phones, and Gasoline,* offering readers a guide to navigating its exploration of global trade, sustainability, and technological evolution.

About the author: Dr. Steven Fawkes

Steven Fawkes is a leading expert in energy efficiency, having dedicated decades to advancing the understanding and implementation of measures that improve energy use across industries. His work has influenced the fields of energy finance, technology innovation, and policy development. Through various platforms, including publications, advisory roles, and public speaking, Fawkes has sought to demonstrate that energy efficiency is not only critical for reducing environmental impact but also offers substantial economic benefits. This summary delves into the key themes of Fawkes' work, including the concept of energy efficiency, its potential for reducing emissions, the financial mechanisms necessary to unlock its value, and the barriers that inhibit its wider adoption.

Energy Efficiency as a Key Strategy for Sustainability

At the heart of Fawkes' work is the belief that **energy efficiency** should be a cornerstone of any sustainable energy strategy. Energy efficiency refers to using less energy to perform the same task or produce the same outcome. This is typically achieved through technological improvements, better management practices, or changes in consumer behaviour. Fawkes emphasizes that improving energy efficiency is one of the most effective ways to reduce greenhouse gas emissions, lower energy costs, and enhance energy security, all while supporting economic growth.

Fawkes argues that energy efficiency is often overlooked in favor of more visible renewable energy projects like solar or wind power. However, he stresses that energy efficiency is "the first fuel," meaning that the cheapest and cleanest energy is the energy that is not used in the first place. This concept underpins much of his work, particularly in advocating for greater investment in energy efficiency measures.

The Economic Case for Energy Efficiency

A significant portion of Fawkes' work focuses on making the **economic case for energy efficiency**. He argues that improving energy efficiency can generate substantial financial returns, both for individual businesses and the wider economy. In many cases, energy efficiency projects offer a high rate of return on investment, with relatively short payback periods. Despite this, businesses and governments often underinvest in energy efficiency due to various market failures and a lack of awareness.

Fawkes has worked to change this perception by promoting **energy performance contracting (EPC)** and other financial mechanisms that can make energy efficiency projects more attractive to investors. EPCs involve energy service companies (ESCOs) implementing energy efficiency measures on behalf of a client and guaranteeing the energy savings that result. These contracts are structured so that the energy savings pay for the cost of the project over time, reducing the financial risk for the client.

Another key area of Fawkes' work is **energy efficiency finance**, which focuses on developing the financial instruments and business models needed to scale up investment in energy efficiency. He emphasizes the need for financial institutions to recognize the value of energy efficiency projects and integrate them into mainstream financing mechanisms. By creating standardized models and risk assessment tools, Fawkes believes that energy efficiency can become a more attractive asset class for investors.

The Role of Innovation in Energy Efficiency

Fawkes is also a strong advocate for **innovation** in energy efficiency technologies and business models. He believes that while many energy efficiency technologies already exist, there is significant untapped potential for further innovation to drive deeper savings. This includes the development of new materials, smart grid technologies, and data analytics that can optimize energy use in real time.

One of Fawkes' key contributions in this area is his emphasis on **"deep energy efficiency"**—a concept that goes beyond incremental improvements to achieve significant reductions in energy use. Deep energy efficiency typically involves a comprehensive approach, addressing multiple aspects of a building or industrial process to maximize energy savings. This contrasts with the more common approach of implementing piecemeal improvements, which may miss opportunities for more substantial reductions.

Fawkes also highlights the role of **digitalization** and **smart technologies** in enabling more effective energy management. The rise of the Internet of Things (IoT), artificial intelligence (AI), and big data analytics has opened new possibilities for monitoring and optimizing energy use. These technologies allow for real-time adjustments in energy consumption, predictive maintenance, and more accurate forecasting of energy needs. Fawkes sees the integration of these technologies into energy efficiency efforts as a crucial next step in maximizing energy savings.

Overcoming Barriers to Energy Efficiency

Despite the clear benefits of energy efficiency, Fawkes acknowledges that there are significant **barriers** to its wider adoption. These barriers include market failures, such as split incentives (where the party responsible for making energy efficiency investments is not the one who benefits from the savings), information asymmetry, and the tendency of businesses to prioritize short-term gains over long-term investments in efficiency.

Fawkes has identified several key strategies to overcome these barriers. One important approach is **raising awareness** about the potential benefits of energy efficiency among decision-makers in both the public and private sectors. Many businesses and governments underestimate the financial and environmental savings that can be achieved through efficiency improvements. Fawkes emphasizes the importance of education and outreach to ensure that these stakeholders understand the full value of energy efficiency.

Another critical factor is the **development of standardized tools and frameworks** for assessing and financing energy efficiency projects. Fawkes advocates for creating clearer metrics and benchmarks that can help businesses and investors evaluate the performance and potential of energy efficiency investments. By reducing uncertainty and providing clear evidence of the benefits, these tools can help overcome the perceived risks associated with energy efficiency projects.

Fawkes also highlights the need for **policy support** to create the right incentives for energy efficiency. This includes regulations and standards that encourage or mandate efficiency improvements, as well as subsidies or tax incentives to reduce the financial burden of investing in energy efficiency technologies. He has worked with governments and international organizations to help design and implement policies that support energy efficiency at scale.

Energy Efficiency in the Global Energy Transition

As the world faces the twin challenges of **climate change** and **energy security**, Fawkes sees energy efficiency as a critical part of the global energy transition. While renewable energy sources like wind and solar are essential for reducing reliance on fossil fuels, Fawkes argues that energy efficiency can deliver significant emissions reductions more quickly and at a lower cost. By reducing overall energy demand, energy efficiency also makes it easier to integrate renewable energy into the grid, as fewer resources are needed to meet total energy needs.

Fawkes' work often focuses on the potential for energy efficiency to deliver **multiple benefits** beyond energy savings. These include improved air quality, enhanced competitiveness for businesses, job creation, and reduced pressure on energy infrastructure. He highlights the importance of recognizing these broader benefits when evaluating the value of energy efficiency projects.

The Future of Energy Efficiency

Looking forward, Fawkes is optimistic about the future of energy efficiency, but he stresses that much work remains to be done. He believes that **scaling up energy efficiency** will require concerted efforts from governments, businesses, and financial institutions. Innovation in technology, financing, and policy will be critical to unlocking the full potential of energy efficiency and ensuring that it plays a central role in the global energy transition.

Fawkes continues to advocate for greater collaboration between the public and private sectors to drive energy efficiency forward. He sees the energy transition as an opportunity to create a more sustainable and resilient energy system, where energy efficiency is no longer an afterthought but a key driver of change. Through continued innovation, investment, and policy support, Fawkes believes that energy efficiency can deliver substantial environmental and economic benefits for decades to come.

In summary, Steven Fawkes' work on energy efficiency has had a significant impact on both the practical implementation of efficiency measures and the broader conversation about how to transition to a more sustainable energy system. By emphasizing the economic, environmental, and social benefits of energy efficiency, Fawkes has helped make the case for its role as a key solution to global challenges like climate change, energy security, and economic growth. His contributions in the areas of finance, innovation, and policy have laid the groundwork for a future where energy efficiency is fully integrated into global energy strategies.